History Lesson

History

A Race Odyssey

Lesson

Mary Lefkowitz

Yale University Press   New Haven and London

For John P. Rosenthal, in memoriam

Published with assistance from the Kingsley Trust Association
Publication Fund established by the Scroll and Key Society of Yale College.

Set in Adobe Minion type by Duke & Company, Devon, Pennsylvania.
Printed in the United States of America.

Library of Congress Cataloging-in-Publication Data
Lefkowitz, Mary R., 1935–
History lesson : a race odyssey / Mary Lefkowitz.
      p.   cm.
Includes bibliographical references and index.
ISBN 978-0-300-12659-4 (alk. paper)
1. History—Study and teaching (Higher)—Massachusetts. 2. Postmodernism and higher education. 3. Racism in higher education. 4. Antisemitism
in higher education. 5. Academic freedom. 6. Wellesley College.
7. Lefkowitz, Mary R., 1935– I. Title.
D16.2.L44 2008
907.1′17447—dc22   2007043532

A catalogue record for this book is available
from the British Library.

The paper in this book meets the guidelines for permanence
and durability of the Committee on Production Guidelines
for Book Longevity of the Council on Library Resources.

10 9 8 7 6 5 4 3 2 1

Contents

vi   *Contents*

Introduction

Would you mind if I began this book with a little quiz? Which of these statements is most controversial?

(a) Greek philosophy was stolen from the Egyptians.
(b) Greek philosophy was borrowed from the Hebrews.
(c) Greek philosophy was invented by the Greeks.

The answer is (c), even though it is the only one of these statements that is backed up by strong evidence. The Greeks were indeed the first ancient people to use philosophy; they were the first to use non-theological language to describe first causes. There is no question about that. Thirty years ago no one would have doubted it. But in the 1990s

I got into a lot of trouble for supporting this traditional view, perhaps precisely because it was the traditional view.

This is the story of how I came to find myself in a controversy for defending an obvious truth. You might be surprised that telling the truth should create a problem in an American university. In the last thirty years or so, however, I have found there to be a kind of moral or ethical confusion among academics, as if we have forgotten what universities are for, or what we were originally hired to do. Telling the truth, instead of being our first responsibility, had suddenly become less important than achieving social goals. These goals were to be reached not by means of the usual scholarly tools of reflection and reasoned persuasion. They were to be imposed by assertion and fiat. Teaching our students and ourselves how to evaluate ideas and evidence or learning how to add to the body of knowledge seemed to me, as I struggled with the events that are the subject of this book, to be no longer top priority.

When my troubles began, I was teaching classics at Wellesley College, as I had done for the previous thirty years. I was (or so I thought) a respected member of our faculty, and reasonably well known as an author and reviewer of books about the ancient Greek world. I became an academic because I loved school. I loved to read, especially about what happened in the past. But what I liked most of all was Latin, because through it I could understand the origin of so many English words, and the structure of grammar. Latin led me to ancient Greek, and that seemed even more exciting. Through it I felt that I was establishing a kind of contact with a past culture that had so much to teach me.

I studied Greek and Latin at Wellesley College, and then

went on to Radcliffe College (the women's college within Harvard) to get my Ph.D. I returned to Wellesley to teach part-time while I was still at graduate school, and stayed on when a full-time position became available. For me it was the fulfillment of a dream. The Wellesley campus is situated in a corner of a leafy suburb of Boston, on one side of a tranquil lake, in a beautifully landscaped park. The buildings look out over trees and woods, with the lake glistening in the distance. I can understand why in the late nineteenth century students wrote serenades to the lake. I have never been able to tear myself away.

Although the campus still looks much the same from the outside, and it remains, by choice, a college for women, over the fifty years that I have known it virtually everything else in it has changed, much of it for the better. The curriculum is richer and more diverse; the students now come from a wide variety of backgrounds and ethnicities, and not just from the suburbs of big cities like Boston or Chicago. The faculty, too, are now more diverse, with a much wider span of interests, and from many different graduate programs. But greater diversity brought a new set of challenges. Old assumptions are today often, some might say endlessly, questioned, but at the same time there is less common ground from which to derive constructive answers. Faculty in the early twentieth century had all grown up reading the same books and had some understanding of what their colleagues in other fields were doing, because in many ways there was less to know. But whole new fields of study exist today that were not even imagined in the 1950s, and instructors in all disciplines are more highly specialized. There are no common texts, and there is less mutual understanding among the disciplines.

Before the twentieth century the study of Greek and Latin had occupied a central place in the curriculum. Over the years increasing demands for relevance in education had gradually driven the study of classics into an honorable niche. For those of us who still cared about the field, our marginalization was at once a disadvantage and an opportunity. The role of a classics professor, as I saw it, was to explain to students why it still made sense to try to learn difficult ancient languages and to study ancient civilizations so different from the world in which we now live. I used my introductory course in Greek mythology to give them an elementary knowledge of Greek religion, with its tragic vision of human life and its acute awareness of the limits of human intelligence.

Mythology is one of the ancient Greeks' most influential legacies. So too, not coincidentally, is its antithesis—an empirical, logical, and abstract system of reasoning that we now call philosophical. Much of my research and writing has focused on the ways in which myth and empirical reasoning intersect in ancient Greek historical writing, and this is probably why, to me, it seemed only natural to want to find out why some people firmly believed that Greek philosophy was stolen from Egypt, even when it so obviously was not.

Perhaps I should have realized that it is one thing to investigate the origin and meaning of myths composed by people who have for centuries been dead and buried, but quite another to critique a contemporary myth that living people today take very seriously. Anyone who tries to teach science in the presence of Creationists will know what I mean.

Challenging a belief system was only part of the problem.

What I'd done, without quite realizing it, was to walk into an intellectual storm that had been raging for some time. The storm had been created (so to speak) by two different weather systems on American campuses, one intellectual and one primarily political. Each was powerful in its own right, but together they transformed themselves into a virtual blizzard. This superstorm changed the quality of discourse in the educational world. Over the past decade or so, it changed it so radically that it was at times hard even for an insider like myself to understand what was happening. Here the weather metaphor breaks down, because this intellectual turbulence was much more durable than a physical storm. It has continued unabated for almost a decade.

This intellectual storm was fueled by what has come to be known as postmodernism. Essentially postmodernism is a form of skepticism combined with self-consciousness. Its adherents believe that no historical narrative can be considered authoritative, because writers always have political motives, whether they are aware of them or not.[1] Postmodernists, in short, believe that there is no such thing as objectivity. Every claim is suspect, especially if it is generally accepted as true. The motives of every historian must therefore be scrutinized, except those of postmodernists themselves.

In its more moderate forms, postmodernism provided a useful corrective to an overconfidence that appeared to have caused the contributions of minorities and women to have been overlooked, especially in the field of American history.[2] But in its more extreme and antirealist forms, postmodernism seemed to support the idea that facts are really nothing more than opinions, that true objectivity is impossible, and that there is no such thing as truth but only a majority opinion, or a dominating consensus, in any particular field of inquiry. At the height of the fad for postmodernism in the 1980s and early 1990s, the very foundations of knowledge seemed to be crumbling; new narratives, new histories needed to be written.

At some point this intellectual storm merged with a political one, in particular a new awareness of racism. Almost everyone in the United States has been affected in some way by racism. The terrible history of racism in this country has generated, and rightly so, deep feelings of guilt among almost all people who might have committed a racist act themselves, or whose parents or ancestors might have been involved in perpetuating a system that encouraged the despicable notion of racial inferiority.

Almost all academics, myself included, have been eager to do whatever they can to right the wrongs of the past in the educational world. Affirmative action and equal opportunity programs were a first step in the long process. University curriculums now regularly include courses that consider the cultures and contributions of different minority groups or investigate the roles minorities played or might have played in contexts where their presence had not previously been remarked. Some minority groups have been granted privileges not available to the majority.

At Wellesley, for example, the Black Task Force (which includes staff as well as faculty) has the right to appoint one of its members to serve on any college committee, a perquisite not granted to any other ethnic group. We have a department of Africana Studies, which in fact I helped to found, back in the days when it was called Black Studies. All faculty members in that department are of African descent. Although no other student organizations are permitted to refuse to take members because of race, religion, or creed, the black student organization Ethos is permitted to limit its membership to students of African descent only.

In addition to these compensatory policies, academics marshaled postmodernism as yet another weapon in what they regarded as their fight against racism. Postmodernism's antirealist approaches have the distinct advantage of being open and available to anyone in virtually any discipline. Academics who adopt these approaches often contend that facts are usually nothing more than statements of a majority or conventional opinion. This belief leads them to conclude that virtually all accounts of the past need to be reexamined or completely recast, because they must be presumed to have been written by authors who were racists, however unwittingly.

One of the great appeals of this approach to history writing is how much it would seem to empower its practitioners. Academics who ordinarily spent their lives sitting on the sidelines observing the action could now play the role of judges, calling past scholars to account, even if their crimes had been committed long ago or until now escaped notice. In this way postmodernist academics became heady with the thought that historical narratives were now not just dusty archives of interest only to specialists, but powerful political tools that could be used to change the status quo, or to bring about needed social reforms.

That myths are now being taught as history has a lot to do with postmodernism. If a myth serves a useful social purpose, or uses the past as a means of righting wrongs in the present, many academics do not want to object to its presence in the curriculum.

For that reason, the book *I, Rigoberta Menchú* has had in recent years a great vogue on college campuses.[3] The book is supposed to be the autobiography of an Indian woman in Guatemala. It has been studied in many classes as if it were a historical document. Largely on the basis of the book's account, its author, Rigoberta Menchú, received the Nobel Peace Prize in 1992.

But in fact the narrative was constructed from audiotapes recorded by the book's editor, and Menchú could not have done all that she claims to have done in the book. Yet her story was, by and large, not questioned by many people. Why? Because it appealed to those who considered it an archetypal narrative of the fate of natives at the hands of colonialists. These enthusiasts preferred to honor the text as such without raising uncomfortable questions about its provenance, factuality, or authenticity. In a sense it was like the partially fictionalized autobiography *A Million Little Pieces* by James Frey, except that in Menchú's case some academics preferred the fiction.[4]

I learned about the power both of postmodernism and of compensatory politics in the early 1990s, after I discovered, to my surprise and dismay, that some members of the Wellesley faculty firmly believed in the theory that Greek culture had been stolen from Africa. In Wellesley's Africana Studies Department, Professor Anthony C. Martin had for many years been teaching his students that theory in his course called Africans in Antiquity. I had always assumed, or wanted to assume, that this course was about the early history of Africa. In practice, I now saw, the course paid special attention to the role of Africans "in Greece and Rome," even though the historical record leaves little doubt that there were few Africans in Greece or Rome and that their cultural influence on these civilizations was negligible. Students were asked to read materials about ancient Egypt, the race of the ancient Egyptians, and *Stolen Legacy,* a book that taught that Greek philosophy and culture had been stolen from Africa—and in particular, literally stolen by Aristotle from the great library at Alexandria, in Egypt.[5]

If Martin's students were being told that this thesis was true, and believed it, then they might also be ready to believe that classical scholars like me who denied it were ignorant of the truth (or worse, were determined to conceal it). But, simply put, the notion is just plain wrong. Aristotle could not have stolen his ideas from the library at Alexandria, because it was built after his death. Nor is there any lack of historical certainty about the dates of the building of the library or of Aristotle's lifespan. These are facts that can be found in any decent reference work or reliable book on the ancient world (and are covered in much more detail in my book *Not Out of Africa*).[6]

But as I would soon discover, it was not historical reality that mattered to Tony Martin or his faction. What mattered to them was simply race. Egypt was a country in Africa, so many people of African descent believed that the ancient Egyptians were an African people. On the other hand, most people of European descent did not consider the question of the "race" of the Egyptians a topic of central interest, and this lack of concern about race was seen as yet another illustration of how historical writing was and is subject, always and inevitably, to prejudice and distortion.

If whites were the majority, and they wrote the histories, weren't those histories virtually predetermined to be racist? The suggestion was not implausible. Until relatively recently, most classical scholars and ancient historians had been white men of European descent. These earlier scholars had failed to take much interest in the roles played by women in ancient societies. Similarly, Egyptologists at the time seem to have been less interested in ancient Egypt's connections with its African neighbors than in its relation to Near Eastern cultures and Greece.

It was certainly justifiable to call attention to these omissions, as many recent scholars have done, and to try to offer a more inclusive and multicultural account of ancient civilizations in the eastern Mediterranean. But what Tony Martin appeared to be teaching his students at Wellesley was that traditional historians of the ancient world were flatly lying. At this point it seemed to me that a response was required.

One of my African-American students advised me not to get involved, particularly in matters concerning Martin. "Don't get into it," she told me; "don't have anything to do with him! You'll just get in trouble." Before the student came to Wellesley her mother had warned her explicitly not to take any courses with Martin.

I certainly never relished the prospect of racial or political controversy. What I have enjoyed most throughout my life is trying to understand the ancient world as best I could from the evidence that is available. I have also tried to get my students to be able to enter that world in their turn. But now I saw that the past could not serve as a refuge. The politics of the present had intruded. I decided I had to speak up, my student's and my misgivings notwithstanding.

My colleagues had reason to wonder why I would choose to get involved in such a thorny issue. They reminded me that the myths I was concerned about had been taught as history for many years on our campus.

At first I was a little shocked by this attitude. My answer was that universities should not support the teaching of demonstrable falsehoods. Even though it might have given some students pleasure to hear that Greek philosophy had been stolen from Africa, by being fed this misinformation they were being shortchanged of the kind of education they were entitled to receive, an education that was supposed to teach them to reason from evidence and to think critically and independently. Second, the misinformation was in effect a form of slander. It wasn't just that it suggested that traditional ancient historians and classicists were lying, or racists, when they weren't. It implied that the ancient Greeks did not deserve credit for their own achievements.

Other ethical issues were involved as well, and I soon discovered that many of these had not been addressed in recent years, so we hardly knew how to define or describe them. How should faculty members behave when confronted with something we didn't want to know about? Or with something that we wished were not true? How to respond when the problem wasn't somewhere else, but right at our doorstep? Was our answer really that we should put our heads in the sand so that we couldn't see the problem?

The campus controversy that erupted eventually brought me face to face with the larger question of what exactly is meant by academic freedom. In recent years, academic freedom has been understood to mean that a professor can teach anything he or she wants without interference—provided of course that the professor has tenure. The privilege, rather unfairly, does not extend to faculty members who don't have tenure, who can be fired (or at least suppose that they might be fired) if they say or do anything controversial. But what (if anything) should a university do if a member of its faculty appears to be teaching something that is demonstrably untrue?

I soon discovered that the usual answer to these questions is simply not to acknowledge that anything is wrong, or to give it another name, or to find some reason to keep one's distance from the source of the trouble. By getting involved, I found out just how unwelcome hard questions can be, even in academe. More aggravating still, I found myself having to put forward the kind of arguments I never imagined I would have to make—for example, to justify and explain how it was that I thought I knew something about the ancient world. Why did I object to the notion that Greek philosophy had its origin in Egypt? Was it because I was white? Was it because I was Jewish? In the course of attempting to answer all of these curiously metaphysical questions, I soon found myself a defendant in a lawsuit that took some five years to meander its way through the legal system. Not quite what I expected to encounter toward the end of what had been up till then a productive and enjoyable career!

Nonetheless, the story is not in the end a sad one, for it is, I hope, a story that will show that one can make a difference if one is prepared to ask civil questions and to make reasoned arguments based on verifiable evidence.

Many people have asked me over the years to tell this tale of my strange odyssey among the Afrocentrists in a book. I was at first reluctant to do so, but I eventually became convinced that it was important not only to speak out against the many forces in contemporary America that compromise the goals and principles of liberal education, but also to show that such struggles can actually, sometimes, be won. As Donald Alexander Downs states at the conclusion of his book about the racial troubles at Cornell in 1969, "If liberalism remains silent through guilt, embarrassment, or simple historical exhaustion, we are lost. The university can lead us out of our respective caves only by being true to itself."[7]

Teachers of course need to have freedom to experiment and to test new theories and interpretations. But academic freedom does not give us the right to rewrite history without reference to the known facts—even if by doing so we imagine that we can bring about social improvement. The scientists among us, for example, do not have license to falsify data to achieve desired results. If a scientist in the "hard" sciences does so, he or she is disciplined and even dismissed. It is often more difficult to distinguish between false and true in the writing of history, but it is still usually possible to establish at least the broad outlines, and to give a clear account of the available evidence. Historians do not have the right to invent their own narratives or to misuse evidence. The Holocaust, for example, did actually take place, and the numbers were not less than has been generally supposed. Responsible historians have reviewed this matter objectively, and the claims of Holocaust deniers or reducers are not supported by the available evidence.

Even if we cannot always find out exactly what happened in the past, we must try to be as objective as we can, even if we can never completely succeed. That is what I have tried to do in this book, drawing whenever possible on published materials that readers can check and verify for themselves.

During the course of this controversy I was accused of racism, conservatism, intellectual naiveté, and the like. Obviously such charges (however undeserved) can be distinctly painful, and it is for that reason that they have been used to such great effect in the culture wars. But the purpose of this narrative is not to catalogue the miseries of being on the receiving end of verbal abuse. Rather, my aim is to describe and expose some of the strategies and arguments that were used to turn an uncontroversial statement about history into a controversy about race and, even beyond that, into an inquiry about the purpose of education. My aim has been to use my experience to show why it is better in the end for all of us to pay attention to facts, and argue from evidence.

That is the ultimate history lesson of the title to this book.

CHAPTER ONE

A Racist Incident?

W henever I think about it, which is often, it becomes harder to imagine how Wellesley College could have been the setting for the controversy that I shall describe in this book. But in 1991 an incident took place there that had a long-lasting and corrosive effect on all of us. Most incongruously, it happened in a residence hall built in high College Gothic style on a hill overlooking a tranquil lake. The leaded windows and carved woodwork in the dormitory's public rooms are intended to draw one away from the present day into an imagined past. It is easy to forget that the city of Boston is only some sixteen miles away.

On the evening of October 30, 1991, the Shakespeare Revelers, a group of students and faculty, met in the living room of

Claflin Hall for a reading of Shakespeare's *Twelfth Night*. Around nine-thirty, the professor who was reading the role of Duke Orsino stepped out to go to the men's room, which was situated halfway down the staircase that led from the first floor to the basement. As he left the men's room and walked back up toward the living room, some students who had been meeting on the lower floor were also coming up the stairs. One of them, Michelle Plantec, an officer of the dorm, asked him politely: "Excuse me, sir, who are you with?" It is an established rule of this women's college that students in residence halls must ask unescorted male visitors to identify themselves.

The professor, Anthony C. Martin, was at the time just over fifty. He is a tall man, invariably well groomed and elegantly dressed. A more experienced student might have guessed that he was a lawyer or a doctor, someone's father, or possibly a professor; that student might have put the question a different way, on the assumption that this clearly respectable man had lost his way in the labyrinth of the residence hall: "May I help you, sir?" Perhaps this phrasing would have elicited a different response. But instead the young woman asked the generic question students are supposed to ask of all male visitors: "Excuse me, sir, who are you with?" Martin answered by asking another question: "What do you mean?" The student replied: "What Wellesley student are you with?"

If Martin had been a different sort of person, he might have explained that he was a professor who was taking part in a play reading in the living room, and that because he had been a member of the faculty for nineteen years, he knew the rules and had asked permission of the receptionist to use the men's room.

The student would then have apologized and continued on her way upstairs. But instead a serious misunderstanding occurred, harsh words were spoken, and the police were called. Apparently Martin had interpreted the student's question as an act of racism. He is black and Plantec is white.

About six months later, three students from a campus literary magazine interviewed Plantec and Martin, who offered different accounts of what had happened.[1] Plantec said: "[Martin] exploded and called me a fucking bitch, a racist, and a bigot, among other things."[2] She said that she then tried to explain to him that the dorm policy allows no guest to go unescorted. Other people gathered around, and someone explained that Professor Martin had indeed asked permission of the student receptionist to go to the men's room without having someone escort him to the door. Meanwhile, the head of house called the police. As Plantec remembered it:

> Martin's reaction was very violent. I don't know how to express how violent his reaction was. Plus, he is a very tall man and he was towering over me, pointing down into my face, and he wasn't saying very nice things. I was very scared and shaking.[3]

When Martin was interviewed, he spoke of being "rudely accosted by a group of women who were coming up the stairs" behind him, whom he tried to ignore. It was only when he got to the top of the stairs that "I became very annoyed and I expressed my annoyance to the people who were behind me."[4] He went back to the living room, where the Shakespeare Revelers were having a reception. The police came and left; no one filed a formal complaint.

What had angered him, Martin said, was the manner in which the students had spoken to him. "I don't take kindly to being approached in a hostile, offensive manner. I don't think anybody does," he said. As he saw it, he had been in a public area of the residence hall, and was clearly *not* trespassing. He added: "I also saw this in the context [of] an atmosphere of bigotry which, unfortunately, pervades this campus and has pervaded this campus for a very long time."[5] Although he denied having used any obscene language, he acknowledged that he had told Plantec that she was a bigot and a racist.[6]

Perhaps if some dispassionate person had been present at the scene, such as an ombudsman or student dean or a member of the clergy, he or she might have been able to soothe both parties and reassure them that it was merely a misunderstanding, an overreaction on Martin's part to an overly zealous student. She or he might have observed that since Martin was the older and presumably wiser party, and an educator by profession, he might have tried to explain to the student how he could have been offended by her question. But no one came forth to serve as mediator; no god appeared from the machine, as they often do at the end of a Greek drama, to tell everyone what to think and what to do. In real life the right person in the right place is rarely there at the right time.

In 1991 there were no clear protocols about how to handle such an incident. According to Plantec, Martin had returned to the Shakespeare group and told them that the only reason she had stopped him "was because he was black." Plantec sought to be exonerated from the charge of racism. The Claflin head of house talked to the dean of students; Plantec called the dean of the college, Dale Rogers Marshall. Marshall in turn referred her to Gwenn Bookman, assistant to the president.[7]

Bookman was well qualified to deal with the issue, since she was a lawyer and advised the college on affirmative action issues. As a black woman, she was well aware of the kinds of misunderstandings that can arise. Bookman wanted to arrange a meeting between Martin and Plantec. But meanwhile Martin, according to his own account, "formed a group" of faculty members who had been present at the play reading, plus some key members of the black community, including the chairman of the Africana Studies Department and the head of the black student organization Ethos.[8]

Plantec wanted to have the meeting that Bookman proposed. The president of the college, Nannerl Keohane, suggested instead that she and Martin meet with a mediator. Neither type of meeting took place. Plantec's father wrote Martin a letter, which (according to Plantec) Martin brought to a meeting of Ethos, where it was read out loud.[9] The Ethos students learned that Plantec was receiving psychiatric care, and that the college had given her one thousand dollars to cover its cost. Plantec was unable to sleep and moved out of her own room into a friend's room. She had a nervous breakdown and went home before exams in mid-December.[10]

In February 1992, soon after Plantec returned to college for the second semester, she heard that Martin had told a student group at a Black History Month event that she was receiving psychiatric care. At dorm meetings Ethos students lectured her on the difficulties encountered by black males on campus. Then she learned that she had not been reappointed as a dorm officer because she would not be an effective representative for "all members of her floor," meaning, presumably, non-whites. Plantec felt that she had been slandered; her father demanded a public apology. Keohane proposed that Martin offer a private apology, but Martin considered the request for either a public or a private apology "unreasonable." He did not apologize.[11]

Plantec left campus in mid-March, without completing her work for the semester.[12] On March 20, 1992, Keohane wrote Martin about "your unwillingness to demonstrate any concern for Michelle Plantec" and "your continuing mockery of her and discussion of the situation with other students." She threatened to "institute disciplinary proceedings against you" if "in future there are confirmed reports of your losing your temper and behaving abusively towards any member of this community."[13] But by then Plantec had left Wellesley, never to return.

No faculty member or group supported Plantec in her quest for a meeting with Martin, because few people were aware of what had happened. No faculty members had witnessed the incident, and the ones who were present at the play reading had first heard about it from Martin. No account of the event appeared in the weekly student newspaper, the *Wellesley News.* The students who conducted the interviews with Plantec and Martin in March 1992 did not publish them until May 1993, when they were about to graduate, some eighteen months after the incident took place. Even then the interviews were printed not in the *Wellesley News,* which is widely distributed on campus, but in *Galenstone,* a student literary magazine that appears on an irregular schedule and in a much smaller print run.

Jennifer Paull, '93, the student editor of *Galenstone,* sought to present the event and its repercussions as "an example of the underlying racial tensions too often overshadowed by the 'polite' environment" of the college community. Paull spoke of "an inherent reluctance to confront racial strain," and she charged that the administration was attempting "to silence" Plantec and Martin to avoid trouble. She called for frank and open discussion of this incident and other racial matters.[14]

Paull and her colleagues deserve great credit for making it possible for others to see that something significant had happened in the residence hall on October 30, 1991. They were undoubtedly right to view it as a *racial* issue, because that is what it had turned into by the time they conducted the interviews. What they did not notice was that it had become a racial issue only because that is how Martin had characterized it. Plantec believed she had stopped him because he was a man in a women's residence hall. Yet Martin's view of the situation appeared to have been given precedence over hers.

Evidently the racial politics of the time made it virtually impossible not to read race into any incident where it might possibly have some relevance. To put it another way, any incident in which a black person was involved tended to be interpreted as a racial issue first and foremost, whether or not there were other, and possibly more significant, ethical issues involved. Martin made a particular effort to tell his version of the story. He talked about the incident with the members of Ethos, who are exclusively black. The faculty members who had been at the play reading with him went to the college president to speak on his behalf, citing other incidents in which campus police and other officials had singled out black men for questioning.[15]

Martin, in addition to being a tenured member of the faculty, was by training a lawyer. He knew how to get across his point of view, and to whom. He could express himself clearly and with authority. Plantec, on the other hand, was a student, young, and far away from her home in a Western state. Another type of person, one who was involved in campus politics, say, might have known how to rally support for herself. But Plantec was primarily interested in science; she was planning to become a doctor.

She had no special advocacy group on campus to draw on. There was of course no such thing as a White Task Force, because it was assumed that no one in the majority culture needed to be defended. Although she was Jewish, she did not choose to identify herself with the Wellesley chapter of Hillel or any student ethnic group. Her only possible defenders, the members of the administration charged with student affairs and racial affairs, sought to act not as advocates but as intermediaries and advisers to both her and Martin.

In retrospect, it seems fair to wonder what would have happened if she had asked a white man what he was doing in a residence hall at night, and he had lashed out at her for accosting him. Surely, virtually any administrator or student on campus would have been sympathetic to her because she had stood up against a male who might have been a potential predator. Around the same time a white male faculty member had almost lost his job because someone claimed to have seen him brush a crumb off a student's face at a party. But for a white student to ask a question of a *black* male was altogether another matter. Every other ethical issue occasioned by the incident paled before that of race. The fate of a particular individual was judged less significant than the attempt in a general way to right the wrongs of the past.

So Tony Martin survived the incident unscathed, and Michelle Plantec had a nervous breakdown and lost a year in her progress toward her medical career. This talented young person left Wellesley, where she was doing well and had enjoyed the support of her peers, because she asked a question of a visitor in a residence hall, one that she had been instructed to ask. Jennifer Paull and the other student interviewers were not comfortable with that outcome, nor should they have been. In this they appeared to differ from the Wellesley administration, which seemed to place a higher priority on "moving on." I shared Paull's discomfort, and the same sense of moral unease compelled me to write about the incident, even though I did not learn about it until more than a year after it happened.

Why did members of the black community accuse Plantec of racism not for what she actually said but for what she *might have meant* when she said it? Certainly it is understandable that they thought racism might have been involved, because black men have all too often been subject to suspicion and special scrutiny. That was a perfectly plausible hypothesis. All the same, is it fair to judge someone on the basis of one person's interpretation of her action rather than on the basis of the action itself? Martin, by his own admission, said things to her that are offensive by any standard when he called her a "racist" and a "bigot."

Perhaps the most celebrated case of a university taking action for perceived verbal abuse occurred some fifteen months after the Plantec incident. This was the so-called water buffalo affair at the University of Pennsylvania, where late one night in

1993, a group of fifteen to twenty women from a black sorority were singing, shouting, and stamping noisily just outside a high-rise residence hall. Some students in the dorm were disturbed by the noise and shouted racist epithets at them. Eden Jacobowitz, a freshman who was in the dorm trying to study, shouted out to them from his window, "Please be quiet." When the noise didn't stop, he shouted again, "Shut up, you water buffalo." Since they were singing about having a party, he suggested that they go to the zoo less than a mile away. The women understood "water buffalo" to be a term of racial abuse.[16]

There was a hearing, in which it was found that "there was 'reasonable' cause to believe that Jacobowitz had violated Penn's racial harassment policy."[17] He was given a choice of accepting a "settlement" or of facing a disciplinary hearing and sanctions that might include suspension or expulsion from the school. He refused to accept the settlement, against the advice of his faculty adviser. Instead he asked history professor Alan Charles Kors to help him, because he had read an article on free speech by Kors and believed that he could stand up to the administration. Eventually it was established that "water buffalo" was not a specifically racial insult. Jacobowitz, an orthodox Jew, had merely been translating into English the Hebrew slang term *behema,* which means a thoughtless or rowdy person, and can often be used affectionately; it was not the sort of word that was intended to "wound." Eventually, Penn dropped the charges against Jacobowitz, but without apologizing in any way for how he had initially been treated.[18]

At Wellesley, Plantec had not been so fortunate, even though she had never said a single word that could have been deemed offensive under the most stringent of speech codes—and in fact Wellesley had no speech code for her to violate. Instead, she was judged on the basis of such intangible and subjective values as tone and intention. Because Plantec did not consult a lawyer or enlist the support of a faculty adviser who could have given her the kind of expert support that Kors provided for Jacobowitz, her case never received the scrutiny that it deserved.[19]

Nonetheless, thanks to the determination of the three students who published the interviews, the issues raised by the incident were brought to the attention of the larger college community. Ultimately, there were significant repercussions, and serious conversations about race were no longer postponed. There was to be progress in a general way, but, alas, no real exoneration for Plantec. Even now, all these years later, I still wonder how such a thing could have happened at Wellesley, where we claim to offer support and guidance for individual students, and where we pride ourselves on being a multicultural community, with all the values of tolerance and understanding that the term implies. The answer, I fear, lies in that moral confusion I have already described, the high priority almost invariably given to certain abstract social goals— or rather, to new prejudices that arose from them. Blame also rests in the confused contemporary belief that all narratives have the same merit. All narratives do not have equal value, because there are such things as facts. Narratives are "equal" only in the sense that all narratives are equally deserving of a hearing. Here, indeed, was the very same confusion that has attended so many of our society's discussions about equality in recent years—about race, about merit, and about "rights" to certain outcomes, instead of to the "equal opportunity" self-evidently due to all.[20]

CHAPTER TWO

Discovering Afrocentrism

ot long before the incident in Claflin Hall, I had started to work on a lengthy review article. Reviewing books is not usually a dangerous occupation. At worst, one can incur the undying enmity of the author whose work one has regarded with less than wild enthusiasm. But this review soon got me into hot water. The literary editor of the *New Republic,* Leon Wieseltier, had asked me to write a review of a new volume of Martin Bernal's *Black Athena* along with a few other titles.[1] Bernal was a professor of government at Cornell, by training a sinologist, who had recently begun to write about the ancient history of the eastern Mediterranean. I wasn't sure I wanted to take on such a big project during the fall term, when I always had a particularly demanding teaching schedule, but Wieseltier persuaded me to try. It was, after all, an unusually timely subject. How often does a book about ancient history speak to the racial politics of our own time?

The first volume of *Black Athena* had come out four years earlier, in 1987, and I'd skimmed through it at the time but hadn't taken it very seriously. It was clear from what Leon was telling me, though, that many other people had taken it very seriously indeed. Excerpts from the book had been published in the British newspaper *The Observer*. The work had sold remarkably well for a book about the ancient world—outstripped, perhaps, only by that perennial best-seller the Bible. Now a second volume had been published. And then there were all those other books that he wanted to send me.

Wieseltier saw that there was a connection among those books. *Black Athena*'s principal thesis was that Greek culture was heavily dependent on earlier cultures in Egypt and the Near East. The rest of the books in the pile he sent also argued that Greek culture had been stolen or borrowed from Egypt, and that the inhabitants of ancient Egypt were Africans. Bernal claimed that that quintessential Greek goddess Athena could be called black because her name was derived from that of the Egyptian goddess Neith.[2] Classical scholars, he believed, because of their racism and anti-Semitism, had failed to acknowledge the full extent of this dependency. Bernal also proposed that Egypt had actually invaded Greece during the second millennium B.C. and that there was a large component of Egyptian vocabulary in ancient Greek, but that it had not been recognized because traditional scholars wished only to stress the connections of ancient Greek to the "Aryan" languages of the Indian subcontinent and of Europe.

At first I wondered why Bernal focused on Egypt rather than the Near East, where the evidence of cultural borrowings was stronger and easier to document. The other books supplied the answer. In them I discovered that there was a longstanding myth, or tradition, claiming that Greek civilization had been borrowed or even stolen from Egypt and that the inhabitants of ancient Egypt were Africans.[3]

One of the books, *Stolen Legacy,* had been in print in various editions for more than forty years. In another, strikingly titled *Africa: Mother of Western Civilization,* Dr. Yosef A. A. ben-Jochannan charged that Aristotle had stolen his philosophy from works by Egyptians in the library of Alexandria. This assertion was obviously false, because the library at Alexandria was not built until after Aristotle's death, and no ancient writer records that Aristotle ever went to Egypt. But despite this and many other obvious problems with the idea of a significant Greek dependence on Egypt, it was clear that thousands of people firmly believed in these ideas and regarded the existence of Greek philosophy as yet another case of a colonialist European plundering of Africa.

If the tradition of a Stolen Legacy was so important, I wondered how it could be that I had never heard of it when I was studying ancient Greek history in graduate school or in the course of some thirty years of teaching. Suddenly I realized that in fact I had heard of it, without quite understanding its significance. A few years earlier a student in my Plato class had complained that I had not pointed out that Socrates was black. At the time, I replied that this was because he wasn't black. He was an Athenian citizen. That meant that both his parents had to have been Athenian citizens, and in turn their parents had to have been Athenian citizens. Foreigners, meaning people from elsewhere even in the Greek world, were excluded from the close-knit kinship groups to which Socrates and other Athenian males belonged.

Then there was a student who had written to the college newspaper to complain that our department had sponsored a screening of *Cleopatra,* a movie starring Elizabeth Taylor. The role, she thought, ought to have been given to a black woman. My colleague Katherine Geffcken invited the student to discuss the issue and tried to explain to her that Cleopatra was a direct descendent of the Macedonian Greeks who then ruled Egypt. But the student wasn't persuaded. Since no surviving ancient portrait of Cleopatra gives any indication of her skin color, the student told Geffcken she would continue to believe what she chose. I had then thought no more about the matter, until I began to work on the review.

After I thumbed through my pile of books, it became clear to me that *Black Athena* was much more than just another book with an interesting theory about the origins of Greek civilization. A whole group of people, including some at my own elite campus, regarded it as scholarly confirmation of the notion that Greek civilization depended on an *African* Egypt. Bernal certainly knew about the tradition of Egyptian priority. He spoke of *Stolen Legacy* as a "fascinating little book" that made "a plausible case for Greek philosophy and science having been borrowed massively from Egypt."[4] Had he heard about the Stolen Legacy theory at Cornell, where he had been a tenured member of the faculty since 1972? The author of *Africa: Mother of Western Civilization,* Yosef ben-Jochannan, known to his followers as "Dr. Ben," had taught part-time at Cornell from 1976 to 1987.[5] Bernal's cleverly chosen title made it clear that the debate was not about ethnicity alone, but also about race.

Race, and the general rancor surrounding everything to do with race, was just one of a number of factors that would make it very hard to respond to Bernal's revisionist history. In the introduction to volume 1 of *Black Athena,* Bernal admitted that his project had a *political* purpose, which was, "of course, to lessen European cultural arrogance."[6] The casual "of course" suggests that Bernal knew that his book would find a sympathetic readership. First, there were the believers in the Stolen Legacy tradition. In addition, there were the academics who had found the thesis of another influential book, *Orientalism* by Edward Said, a convincing one.[7] In it, Said had taken European scholarship of the eighteenth and nineteenth centuries to task for intellectual condescension toward non-Europeans and their civilizations. Said regarded most of Western scholarship as a kind of intellectual colonialism—a view that appeals emotionally to many people, but better applies to tangible artifacts, like the Elgin marbles, than it does to history writing, which is constantly subject to revision and reinterpretation.

Certainly scholarship exists to be scrutinized. Proponents of Afrocentrism or postmodernism or new historicism or any other interpretive theory are quite right to say, for instance, that nineteenth-century scholars far too often regarded Socrates as a precursor of Jesus, or described only the positive side of Athenian democracy while omitting to mention its disenfranchisement of women, slaves, and foreigners. But the trouble was (or so it seemed to me) that Bernal seemed to assume that being European meant that one was automatically culturally arrogant. Did that generalization include everyone? Wasn't it fundamentally racist? Surely some scholars had simply wanted to find out, as best they could, what might have happened in the past.

Now it is true that scholarly study of the past resembles colonialism in that it seeks to explain civilizations of peoples different from ourselves, who sometimes have no power directly to explain themselves to us or to defend themselves against our misinterpretations or to stop us from taking their possessions away to our own countries. But historical scholarship is fundamentally a different kind of enterprise from political or economic colonialism. Scholars do not keep what they find, but give it back freely to all who want to know it. In so doing they also accept all the risks of scrutiny, and criticism for what they have said and done.

As I saw it, Bernal's book presented a serious challenge, both to the basic narrative of ancient history and to the whole purpose of studying the past. If I read him correctly, he was saying that one shouldn't study history to learn what had happened—because it was impossible to discover all the facts, especially in the case of the remote past—rather, the best one could do was to offer a "plausible" account. The role of the historian was to assess the various "competitive plausibilities" and pick the one that was most persuasive.

But how to decide which was the most plausible? Bernal seemed to be saying that the most persuasive narrative was the one with the most desirable result. In effect, he was preaching a kind of affirmative action program for the rewriting of history, a project to revamp the past in order to bring about social change in the present. To Bernal, the Egyptian pharaohs could "usefully" be called black, because, presumably, today a lot of people wanted them to be black.[8] Then he failed to do what scholars are traditionally expected to do: to review all the available anthropological data in the effort to reach an objective conclusion taking account of all the evidence. But he included an extensive bibliography and the learned references that would make his work look comprehensive and authoritative.

I was glad to concede that we could easily think of the ancient Egyptians as an African people. After all, they certainly weren't white-skinned or European. But I was uncomfortable about Bernal's competitive plausibility method, because it was fundamentally subjective. If Bernal or I could simply rewrite history to bring about the social changes we desired (and I felt sure that I hated the racism in American society just as much as he did), then what was to stop the Ku Klux Klan from rewriting history to suit their nefarious purposes?

Bernal seemed to believe it was impossible for anyone, particularly a scholar, to be objective. In volume 2 he stated that he had given up "the mask of impartiality," and that he would from now on argue for his point of view.[9] That he regarded history writing as a form of advocacy was a fact that I found deeply disturbing, even shocking. I had always been taught that a historian must stand aside from his or her material and try to give the most accurate account he or she could of the available facts. Certainly, Bernal's idea of what it meant to be a historian of antiquity (or of anything else) differed greatly from mine, to put it mildly.

In claiming that objectivity was impossible, Bernal was leaning on some powerful and influential allies. The trendy

French theorist Michel Foucault, in books like *Madness and Civilization,* had argued that people in power, and indeed cultures in general, are in a position to determine the nature of reality, and that therefore, any perception of reality is in effect an artificial construction.[10] If the definition of insanity could vary widely from culture to culture and also change over time, how could we be so sure about everything else? Scholars who believed Foucault tended to express deep cynicism about the work of their predecessors. Like Bernal, they were ostentatiously determined to describe their methodologies and to characterize scholars who tried to make sense of the available data as hopelessly naive and unsophisticated. And that, alas, included me.

In some respects, Bernal's views were not all that revolutionary. Challenging conventions has always been a scholarly enterprise. I'd done it often enough myself. I was one of the first scholars in my field to point out how condescending some older commentators had been toward the writing of ancient women poets like Sappho. Although many scholars still relied on ancient literary biographies in their interpretations of ancient poetry, I had written a book that demonstrated that those biographies were fanciful historical fictions.[11] But although I challenged conventional ideas, I still relied on standard methods of research and documentation, and built upon the work my predecessors had done.

What Bernal was trying to do, on the other hand, was to question the whole nature of the discipline, mostly by accusing other scholars of engaging in an enormous cover-up, consciously or unconsciously. He was claiming that the nature of the Greek language and the main outlines of ancient history had been wholly misunderstood—until he came along. What was more, despite his lack of formal credentials in the field, he was being considered authoritative just because he claimed to be attacking racial and religious prejudices.

The entire mode of argument made any reasoned discussion of his work difficult. Any defense of classical scholarship could be accused of apologizing for racists. Any presentation of the available facts—such as the fact that there was no archaeological evidence or linguistic traces to show that Egypt had invaded Greece in the second millennium B.C.—could be dismissed on the ground that there were no such things as facts or objectivity.

The very fact that I was a well-established scholar in my field, for example, was used as an indictment against me. Bernal stated in the introduction to volume 1 that any change in the traditional view of ancient history would need to come from outside the discipline, from scholars like himself, whose expertise was in another academic subject. Classics students, he wrote, "have been so thoroughly imbued with conventional preconceptions and patterns of thought that they are extremely unlikely to be able to question its basic premises."[12] We were intellectually passive. We could translate, but not think.

All I could do was hope someone out there still thought that the facts mattered, and that not all classical scholars were mindless translators of texts, and that some of us were not unduly prejudiced. I wasn't exactly sure how to defend myself against the charge that I, as a classics scholar, was a racist or intellectually passive. You can't just stand up and deny that you are a racist and expect people to believe you just because you are sincere. But I had to try, and I had only a limited amount of time and space to do it in. In addition, I had to explain to a general readership why it was that there was absolutely no reason in the world to believe that Greek philosophy was stolen from Egypt or from anywhere else. It was an exceedingly tall order.

I began my review, which appeared early in 1992, by telling the story of the two students who complained that we hadn't pointed out that Socrates and Cleopatra were black.[13] Had we deceived ourselves? Scholars could certainly be wrong. Until 1952, classicists had believed that the Greek language had not been used in Greece until around 1000 B.C. But then Michael Ventris deciphered clay tablets at Mycenae dating to the middle of the second millennium B.C., which showed that Greek had been spoken there hundreds of years earlier.

Ancient historians rarely have all the facts at their disposal that they would like to have. But nonetheless we did know *something*. If Socrates had been an African his contemporaries certainly would have mentioned it, because there were only a few Africans in Athens at the time, or even in the next several centuries. Every student of ancient art was aware of Egyptian influences on Greek art and architecture, but that did not mean that the artifacts themselves were made in Egypt. Greek culture was divided from Egypt and Africa by language and genealogy. But influence was not necessarily a sign of origin.

Subsequent civilizations always sought to connect themselves with the ancient Greeks, so it was not at all surprising to see that Afrocentric writers also wanted to claim Greece for themselves. Marcus Garvey in 1923 had complained about how white people had always tried to rob black people of their history: "Every student of history, of impartial mind knows . . .

that ancient Egypt gave the world civilization and that Greece and Rome have robbed Egypt of her arts and letters, and taken all the credit to themselves."[14] The Senegalese writer Cheikh Anta Diop, whose work was widely influential in Francophone Africa and was now available in English, wrote about the Greek myths that mention Africa.[15] Diop thought that the legend of Dido, the queen of Carthage, symbolized the way Europeans treated Africans. Dido had been seduced and then abandoned by the Trojan hero Aeneas, the founder of Rome.

Then there were the claims of George G. M. James, the author of *Stolen Legacy*, who believed that Aristotle took his ideas about the soul from the Egyptian Book of the Dead. James said that Plato stole his ideas from other Greek philosophers, who in turn took them from Egypt. In *Africa: Mother of Western Civilization*, ben-Jochannan stated that Aristotle took books from the library of Alexandria and put his name on them. If these writers had been justified in their assertions, why would anyone have continued to study the Greek and Latin classics, at least in the way that they had traditionally been taught? The direct answer to the question was that no one ever *had* taken these claims seriously, until now, because they had no merit.

Discovering the true origins of Greek civilization had been a hard and complex scholarly task accomplished over centuries. Myths had often told of settlers coming from the Near East to Greece, but myths are not easily converted into history. Even Herodotus, the father of history, had his limitations. He reported what the Egyptian priests told him, but did they know what they were talking about? Did he get it right? Even though Herodotus was excited to see resemblances between Egyptian and Greek religious practices, he regarded Egyptian culture as fundamentally distinct from that of Greek-speaking peoples.

Bernal's etymologies in *Black Athena* were questionable, and he tended to read political meaning into works of European fiction. That Egypt had invaded Greece in the second millennium B.C. was highly unlikely, given the total lack of any archaeological or linguistic evidence for such an incursion. There was no historical evidence that the Greeks ever stole anything from Egypt, including their philosophy. Bernal also never came to grips with what the ancients meant by black. Herodotus, for example, distinguished between Egyptians and Ethiopians, the people to the south and west.

Bernal clearly wanted to support the myth of Egyptian priority, regardless of the historical record, because it seemed to him to serve a beneficial social purpose to do so. But he could achieve this goal only by taking from the ancient Greeks their most significant achievements. Here, if anywhere, was the real stolen legacy! What an ironic end for a people who, in their historical and philosophical writings, had always sought to distinguish between fact and fiction. In my view, it was in any case misguided for any modern people to claim the ancient Egyptians or the ancient Greeks as their own property. "All these civilizations," I wrote in the *New Republic* review, "like everything else in the past, belong equally to all of us."

When I look back at the review I wrote for the *New Republic* from a distance of some fifteen years, it seems to me today anything but controversial or incendiary. The tone is calm, and the argument appealed to fact and reason. I did not mention any writer's ethnicity or racial identity. Yet the review made some people very angry, so much that the controversy around these issues continues to this very day. Some complained that I had not defined what I meant by "Afrocentric," so I will do so here. The term refers to those who attempt to rewrite history in order to make Africa play the role in history that had usually been assigned to Europe. As far as I am concerned, neither Afrocentrism nor Eurocentrism is justifiable. Ideas do not travel in one direction only, but back and forth and sideways, especially in the ancient eastern Mediterranean. Others complained that I had implied that Africa had no history, that ancient Egypt hadn't had a high civilization long before the Greeks, or that the ancient Egyptians had not been capable of profound thought. But I certainly had never said any of those things.

Some people were upset because the cover of the *New Republic* in which my essay on *Black Athena* appeared showed in garish black and white and purple a picture of a bust of an ancient philosopher wearing a Malcolm X cap. They thought it improper that a magazine cover seemed designed to shock. I can only say that I was not consulted about the magazine's cover design, and first saw it only when my own copy arrived in the mail. It seemed to me, then as now, no more than a rather tasteless joke. Spike Lee's film *Malcolm X* had just been released, and Malcolm X caps were in fashion. But my critics imagined that the cover was declaring: "Watch out, because the Nation of Islam and radical blacks are destroying Western civilization." Be that as it may, that certainly wasn't what *I* was saying in the article, or even thinking. I don't believe that extreme forms of Afrocentrism, like the Nation of Islam, have ever had the overwhelming support of African Americans in this country.[16]

I was much more worried about what people like Martin Bernal were doing to the study of ancient history. Unfortunately, I did not have space in my *New Republic* review to provide a separate overview of what most of us were teaching. I shall do so here, in order to explain why I found Bernal's approach to the study of the past so profoundly disturbing.

The term "race" is essentially anachronistic. As far as anyone knows, we are all of African origin, because all human life originated on that continent. Over the course of many thousands of years, people migrated to other parts of the world. The differences in appearance among humans today result from centuries of inbreeding.[17]

During the third millennium B.C., Egyptians made clear distinctions between themselves and other peoples, which they represented in their art.[18] Wall paintings are not photographs, and to some extent the different colors may have been chosen as a means of marking nationality, like uniforms in a football game. The Egyptians depicted themselves with a russet color, Asiatics in a paler yellow. Southern peoples were darker, either chocolate brown or black. The name Nubian is based on the Egyptian word for "bronze or burnt," and is analogous to the term that the Greeks used to describe Africans who lived south of Egypt, *aithiops* (burnt in appearance).

That the Egyptians considered themselves distinct from other Africans does not mean that they were not in origin an African people. An Egyptian from ancient Memphis would have had to sit in the back of the bus in Memphis, Tennessee, during the days of segregation.

During this time the ancient Egyptians attained a high

level of civilization. They had a system of writing, built impressive architectural structures, and were adept at certain types of mathematical calculation. They had theories (though not necessarily accurate ones) about the operation of the human body, and recorded their methods for the use of other practitioners.

In the second millennium, invaders from the East began to settle in Asia Minor, the Aegean islands, and mainland Greece. The language these invaders spoke (known in English as Greek) was in origin Indo-European, rather than from the Afro-Asiatic language family whose members include Hebrew and Egyptian. The presence of words in their language that were not Indo-European or of Semitic or Egyptian origin suggests that there already was an indigenous population or populations in the area.[19] These populations appear to have included the so-called Minoans who built communities or palaces on Crete and several Aegean islands. The Minoans recorded what appear to be inventories on clay tablets, but their script language has not yet been deciphered or identified.

The Egyptians were in contact with the inhabitants of the Aegean islands and other early civilizations through trade. During the hegemony of the Semitic "Hyksos" pharaohs (ca. 1650–1550 B.C.), Egyptians in Lower Egypt traded with Cyprus and Crete, and brought Minoan artists from Crete or some other Aegean island to Avaris on the Nile Delta. Some new loanwords made their way into Egyptian as a result of this trade, from both Near Eastern and Indo-European sources.[20] Trade and contact continued after the Greek-speaking people known as Myceneans took over the Minoans' palaces and many aspects of their culture. Neither archaeological nor linguistic evidence offers any indication that Egyptians invaded mainland Greece or the islands.

During the first millennium B.C., there appears to have been little contact between Egypt and Greece following the collapse of Mycenean civilization. But in the mid-seventh century contact between Egyptians and Greeks resumed.[21] The pharaoh Psamtek I Wahibra (664–610 B.C.), called Psammetichus by the Greeks, employed Greek mercenaries. A base for Greek traders was established in the Nile Delta at Naucratis. In 570 B.C. the pharaoh Ahmose II ("Amasis," 570–526 B.C.) also used Greek mercenaries, and in 548 he financed the rebuilding of the temple of Apollo at Delphi.

A few Greek words, mostly technical in character, were adopted into Egyptian at this time, such as *wynn*, the term used to designate all Greeks, from the Greek *hoi Iones* ("the Ionians"). From around 600 B.C. Egyptian architecture and sculpture had a noticeable influence on Greek builders and artists, but the Greeks scaled everything down in size and gave their structures a distinctive appearance.[22] Ideas about life after death may have come to Greece from Egypt around this time, and the indigenous Greek god Dionysus may have acquired some of the characteristics of the Egyptian god Osiris.

Some learned Greeks, like Solon and Thales, may have visited Egypt in the seventh and sixth centuries. After the Persians conquered Egypt in 525 it was difficult for Greeks to travel there, but in the fifth century the Greek historians Hecataeus and Herodotus were able to visit Egypt, because they came from cities in Persian-dominated Asia Minor. Greeks employed occasional Egyptian words in their language for specialized items found in Egypt, such as *baris,* for a special type of Egyptian boat. Most of the loanwords in daily use derived from Near Eastern languages.[23]

The Greeks probably acquired some practical medical knowledge from the Egyptians through their trade connections, but it is more likely that they learned about mathematics and astronomy from the Near Eastern peoples with whom they came into frequent contact.[24] Egyptian mathematics appears to have had very little direct influence on the work of other ancient Mediterranean peoples.

The Greek method of mathematical calculation can be distinguished from that of earlier cultures because of its use of abstract terms.[25] Whereas Egyptian scribes would present a series of related specific calculations (showing that in principle they knew that these all dealt with a related problem), the Greeks developed the use of theorems to express in abstract terms the principle behind the calculations.

In the late sixth and early fifth centuries Greek thinkers in Asia Minor and southern Italy who were critical of traditional mythology came up with non-theological theories of the origin of the universe. But what we now know as Greek philosophy developed in the democracy of ancient Athens, in an atmosphere that supported questioning and debate, by Socrates (469–399 B.C.), his pupil Plato (429–347 B.C.), and Plato's pupil Aristotle (384–322 B.C.), who was born in Macedonia but settled in Athens.

Greeks lived in Egypt after Alexander's conquest, but stayed primarily in Alexandria and kept themselves separate from the native population. From the time of Alexander's conquest of Egypt in 332/1 until 31 B.C., when Cleopatra VII was defeated by the Romans, all of the pharaohs were Macedonian Greeks. Greeks founded the library at Alexandria in about 297 B.C., after Alexander's general Ptolemy I Soter had assumed the role of pharaoh (305–282 B.C.) and established himself in the new city.[26]

In the early centuries A.D., as Christianity spread, a large number of Greek loanwords made their way into the late Egyptian (or Coptic) language, including some words of an abstract nature, like *logikos* ("spiritual"). It was only in the early centuries A.D. that anything like what we think of as Greek philosophy was written on Egyptian soil, such as the Books of Hermes. These works were written in Greek, by writers who had read Plato and Aristotle and their successors, and attempted to make a synthesis of Greek and Egyptian elements. The treatises take the form of a dialogue (or monologues with occasional responses) between a father and son. In the treatises the adviser is Hermes, who is identified with the Egyptian god Thoth.

Egyptologists have now discovered a contemporary dialogue of Hermes/Thoth written in demotic Egyptian. In it, as in the Greek texts, there is a comfortable and loving relationship between the god and his human disciple.[27] In the Egyptian treatise of Thoth, the god Thoth gives advice in a fatherly way, and there is an emphasis on knowledge that one also finds in the Greek dialogues of Hermes, and also common phrases. But the Book of Thoth treats topics that are not mentioned in the Greek texts.[28]

Thoth talks about the Egyptian gods, sacred animals, scribal tools, and a successful journey through the Egyptian underworld for the disciple and his *ba*, or "essence." Existence after death is a constant preoccupation in Egyptian theological writing and funerary art.

In the Hermetic dialogues written in the Greek language, the speakers are not talking about religious tradition, but seeking to describe the nature of divinity in general: "Mind as a whole wholly enclosing itself, free of all body, unerring, unaffected, untouched, at rest in itself, capable of containing all things and preserving all that exists, and its rays (as it were) are the good, the truth, the archetype of spirit, the archetype of soul."[29] It is apparent that Greek was the language even Egyptians were compelled to use if they were going to write anything that resembles what we would now call a philosophical dialogue. Plato and Aristotle were not the beneficiaries, but the source of and inspiration for philosophical works produced in Egypt.

CHAPTER THREE

Two Views of
Ancient History

My concern was about the teaching of ancient history, but hard as I tried to keep race out of the discussion, it soon became the central issue surrounding Bernal's book and my review of it. No doubt the provocative cover of the *New Republic* made that inevitable. Most of the letters I got said nothing about the historical or linguistic questions I had raised. What they cared about was whether Socrates or Cleopatra or other ancients had been black or white. I would have been glad to point out that the color of their skin mattered much less to Cleopatra and Socrates than how they had defined their own ethnicities.[1] Socrates had thought of himself as an Athenian. Cleopatra regarded herself as a Macedonian Greek pharaoh of Egypt.

At first colleagues seemed to have no objections to my article. It was soon used as one of the readings in a discussion group on multiculturalism that the president of Wellesley, Nannerl Keohane, organized.

Perhaps nothing in this book would ever have happened had I been willing to simply shrug my shoulders and accept the fact that the Stolen Legacy theory was being taught as history at Wellesley. But I couldn't. The fact that such nonsense could be purveyed as history disturbed me as much as if I had learned that another Wellesley professor was teaching that the Holocaust had never happened. If someone proposed that we have courses in Creation Science, I would have joined my biologist colleagues in the picket line. One does not have to be a scientist to know that evolution is not just another hypothesis.

Academics often disagree with one another about interpretations and emphasis within their own fields. I was no stranger to such controversies and had often been involved in lively debates within my discipline. We argued at conferences and in learned journals, but we were always cordial to one another in person, and our students learned from the give and take of different arguments.

I thought, then, that raising some questions about the teaching of Afrocentric ancient history would lead to the same kind of fruitful discussion and process of scholarly learning. There were many interesting issues to be considered. What evidence was there that the ancient Egyptians were engaged in the pursuit of what the Greeks called philosophy? Did famous Greek figures study in Africa? Were some of them Africans? Answering those questions would get to the heart of how we think we know what we know.

In retrospect, given the personalities involved, that expectation was hopelessly naive. There was no way here to agree to disagree or to acknowledge respectfully the existence of the others' point of view. If there had been, the debate might have started years earlier. Faculty members in different fields often initiate such dialogues spontaneously when they find that they have overlapping interests. To encourage just such exchanges on a wide variety of subjects, I had a few years earlier helped set up a series of faculty seminars for cross-disciplinary dialogues, and they had so far been a great success.

So my first move was to suggest a faculty seminar on the origins of Greek civilization to talk about Bernal's work and related issues. My ancient history colleague Guy Rogers was enthusiastic, and he joined with Selwyn Cudjoe of our Africana Studies Department in putting together a proposal. But that was just a start, and it wouldn't happen until June.

The question then was what to do about what our students were learning in such courses as Africans in Antiquity. Tony Martin had taught this class for years in the Africana Studies Department. The description in the college catalogue included a reference to "Africans in Greece and Rome." It was hard to see exactly who he had in mind. Socrates? Cleopatra? In reality there isn't much to know about Egyptians, Ethiopians, and other Africans in Greece and Rome (or Italy).[2] Most of the little information we have about them comes from inscriptions on graves and other monuments, few of which have been translated from the original languages.

On the other hand, there was a lot one could say about Africans in the wider Greco-Roman world as a whole, which included Egypt and large portions of northern Africa. So I thought I might suggest that the course description be changed from "Africans in Greece and Rome" to "Africans in the Greek and Roman world," so that at least the public record of what was taught would not be embarrassingly unhistorical. I tried to discuss the proposal with Tony Martin. I sent him a memo about my idea with a copy of my *New Republic* article. He didn't reply. I spoke to him about the possibility of revising the course description. Again, he didn't reply.

So when the whole college curriculum was presented to the entire faculty for discussion during a meeting of the Academic Council, as it is every year, I proposed changing the wording to "Africans in the Greco-Roman world." Martin wasn't present at the meeting, and no one from his department objected.

The motion to amend passed, probably because no one thought that it made much difference one way or the other. But that was not how Tony Martin understood it. He went immediately to Dale Marshall, the dean of the college, and demanded that the original wording be restored. Marshall did as Martin asked, on the grounds that it was merely an editorial change.

Marshall's action was puzzling, because it defied college protocol. When I asked why the original wording had been restored, Dean Marshall told me that Martin had been very angry. When I suggested that the wording the faculty had approved was more accurate historically, she told me: "He has his view of ancient history and you have yours." Did she really suppose that these contradictory views could both be true at the same time?

I was completely unprepared for her response. In fact, I couldn't believe my ears. She had seen my *New Republic* review. Did she still suppose that Martin was teaching a course on the history of Africa in antiquity?

A decade earlier, another dean of the college would have assured me that yes, of course, what Martin was teaching was the myth of the Stolen Legacy, but that there was no point in changing the course description because it would have no effect on what was said in the classroom. That dean might have asked me not to pursue the matter, because it might seem as if I meant to insult Martin personally. I would have understood that the dean was doing her best to keep the peace.

But Dale Marshall had said, and for all I knew, actually *believed,* that both views of the past had equal merit and could comfortably coexist within the same institution. In effect, she was saying that credentials, knowledge of ancient languages, familiarity with archaeological sites, everything I had worked hard for years to acquire, no longer had any intrinsic value. And that was discourteous, insulting, outrageous, even though she didn't seem to know it. Did she and other intelligent people imagine that knowledge was the same thing as opinion? Or that myths could be taught as history, because they might have a redemptive or social value?

Apparently, yes. Not long before, Jerold Auerbach, a history professor, was summoned by Marshall and the college affirmative action officer to answer a student's charge that he had been "hindering diversity."[3] Auerbach argued in class that the Holocaust was unique in human history because it was "the targeted extermination of an entire people." An African-American student in the class "erupted in anger," citing the six million slaves who had died in transit to the Americas. She had a point, which Auerbach might have acknowledged (though in fact the figure was probably more like *one* million). But why was it assumed that Auerbach had *racist* rather than historical motives when he disagreed with a student about the definition of the term "Holocaust"? Auerbach claims that he was able to bring the discussion with the dean and the affirmative action officer to a conclusion only by mentioning academic freedom and "lawyer" in the same sentence.

The idea of promoting diversity in history wasn't restricted to Wellesley. In the 1990s many academics talked not only about evidence but about how the evidence was *presented*. Most of the world's history, it was said, had been written by the winners of wars or at least by their survivors. In our own country the opinions of some groups had always carried more weight than those of others. Didn't we also need to listen to minority voices in history that had not been heard? If there were contradictions among narratives, shouldn't we be willing seriously to consider or at least give the benefit of the doubt to the minority point of view?

By accepting the possibility that an alternative or minority narrative might be valid, Dale Marshall may only have been trying to be fair. But at the time it seemed to me that the dean was simply being political, indeed cynical. She knew Tony Martin was capable of making a lot of trouble for her if she did not go along with what he wanted. He could claim that he was being discriminated against because he was black—indeed, he had already done so. In 1987 he had sued the college for discrimination because he was not satisfied with a routine evaluation of his scholarly work by a faculty committee, and he received a monetary settlement from President Keohane.[4] On the other hand, the dean could be pretty sure that I was unlikely to do anything so disruptive. I was known to be a team player, loyal to the college. I had been treated well and evaluated highly by both administrators and colleagues for many years, and my relations with her had always been cordial.

I couldn't help wondering what Dean Marshall would have said if Tony Martin had suggested a change of wording in one of *my* courses and the Academic Council had approved it. If I'd complained, I'm sure she would have told me that it was too late to change it and that I ought to have objected when the matter first came up. Why hadn't I been at the meeting at which the change was proposed? The wording was voted on now; it was too late for changes; it was all in accordance with the college rules that were clearly printed in the Faculty Handbook. *This* would have been the usual disposition of such matters by the Wellesley administration. But Marshall was not prepared to deliver any such message to Tony Martin, even though, as a faculty member at Wellesley of long standing, he surely knew, or ought to have known, the rules.

It was clear that Tony Martin was being given preferential treatment. What was more, people were afraid of him—in part because he was so much more willing to express his feelings than everyone else, and in ways that almost everyone else at Wellesley, myself included, were not. Every transaction, however unpleasant, was expected to be conducted with utmost civility. Persuasion and reason, I had been taught all my life, were more effective in the long run than threats or displays of emotion. Decisions were to be made by consensus, not by directives and bullying. Now, it seemed, the rules had changed. At least for some people.

That seemed unfair. But what upset me much more was that no one else seemed concerned about whether nonsense and falsehoods were being taught. One of my classics colleagues said defensively, and with apparent reasonableness, "Oh, come on, you know there were some Africans in Greece and Rome." Sure. But there was next to nothing to be said about them. They had left virtually no historical trace. By letting students believe that they had a significant cultural influence on Greek civilization, it seemed to me that we were encouraging our students to believe a lie.

Surely academic freedom had to be protected—but phony history? Universities regularly discipline faculty members who falsify scientific data. But the classroom has so far been considered sacrosanct. I wondered what would happen if some professor were to claim that his class had created a cold-fusion reactor, or that there was no Holocaust.

Presumably one would be more forgiving if the instructor was deluded and sincerely believed that he was conducting experiments using cold fusion. You discuss the evidence with him, but if he still insists that what he is saying is true, what next? This, unfortunately, is a road most administrators would prefer not to go down, because of the high cost of litigation and bad publicity, which might affect university endowments or even college enrollments.

The more I thought about it the less likely it seemed that anyone at Wellesley would ever lift a finger to stop false history from being taught. The only silver lining in this cloud was that if academic freedom protected Tony Martin, it also covered me. That was at least something. If I wanted to, I could continue to speak out.

At some point I found out that Tony Martin had given a lecture to the local chapter of Alpha Kappa Alpha, the black students' sorority, in which he claimed that Aristotle stole his philosophy from Egypt. So I asked the sorority if they would consider letting me speak as well. Martin communicated his disapproval, saying he regarded it as another "very hostile onslaught."[5] An *onslaught?* He regarded discussion as an *invasion?*

Apparently so. Martin continued to use the language of war and passed this same rhetoric on to his students, who in turn would repeat his arguments and rhetoric almost verbatim. Two of Martin's students wrote a letter to the *Wellesley News* complaining about all the "unjust attacks" against the Africana Studies course Africans in Antiquity.[6] I was named as the leader, "a 'scholar' in the Greek Dept., who minimizes the work of any Black scholar regardless of the vast amount of evidence he presents on the African origins of humankind." They concluded with a rousing cheer for ethnocentricity: "You must acknowledge the truth because Black people will not allow you to take away our history. Slavery is OVER!"

They also went out of their way to point out that the writer of a *New York Times* article about black pharaohs from Nubia was *Jewish.* Well, how did they know? And why should it matter? The letter itself seemed that it might have been prepared for the students, for it had been sent, unsigned, from the Africana Studies Department.[7] What did they think the religion or race or ethnicity of a *New York Times* science writer had to do with what he was writing about? What would they have said if a white person had called attention to a reporter's being black if that was irrelevant to the issue being discussed?

Perhaps even worse, the letter showed that, despite their expensive educations, these students weren't being taught how to consider all the available evidence when presenting an argument. They were saying that no history written by white people could be trusted. If anyone had said the same kind of thing about black people it would have rightly been considered racist.

In my response to the *Wellesley News* explaining that the *New Republic* article was not about the Africans in Antiquity course, but about Martin Bernal's *Black Athena,* I tried to show that they had misunderstood what Herodotus was saying in a couple of paragraphs they had cited.[8] As far as slavery was concerned, Orlando Patterson had recently said on our campus, and shown in his newly published book *Freedom,* that Greek writers were among the first people to discuss the evils of slavery.[9]

Nothing I said was untrue, but in retrospect I think the letter had the wrong tone, sounding as if I were talking down to them; perhaps at this juncture I should have tried to reach out and ask them why on earth they thought I or any other classical scholar would want to lie to them, or why they supposed that I was a closed-minded bigot when they hadn't even spoken with me. In fact I did write a personal letter to them a couple of weeks later, saying that I was puzzled by their charges and asking them to help me understand why they wrote what they did about me. But it was too late, and they never replied.

As it happened, the day after the students' letter appeared in the *Wellesley News,* the *Chronicle of Higher Education* featured an op-ed piece that I had written some weeks earlier about the Stolen Legacy myth.[10] I did not mention Tony Martin by name, but I talked about a colleague who told his students that Aristotle stole his philosophy from the library at Alexandria, and wondered why it wasn't possible to discuss the historical issues he had raised. The point of studying ancient culture was not to learn about ourselves, but "to understand the history of civilization, in all its diversity." Afrocentrists like Martin, in appealing to emotions and by refusing even to discuss the issues, were abandoning the rationalist tradition that the Greeks were supposed to have stolen from their ancestors. This statement struck some of my critics as a fundamentally racist claim.

Tony Martin devoted a long section of the spring 1992 Africana Studies Newsletter to an attack on me. He reprinted his students' letter to the *Wellesley News,* saying that his students knew their Herodotus better than I did.[11] I had objected to their assertion that Heracles' parents were of Egyptian origin and that Herodotus wrote about the Egyptian doctrine of the soul. Martin produced quotations to show that Herodotus had used those phrases in his text. Because this statement appeared just before Commencement in a departmental newsletter edited by himself, there was no way for me to point out that the quotations were drawn from a popular but eccentric translation that did not accurately reproduce the sense of the original Greek.

Three classics majors were so upset about the exchange in the *Wellesley News* and what they had been hearing from students in the Africana Studies Department that they went to see President Keohane about the matter. She advised them to consider Tony Martin's feelings. He was on his own, she said, while I had the support of tradition and the classics profession. She had a point, but I couldn't help wondering why we were talking about feelings instead of historical values. Academic values and social progress had come head to head, and academic standards were being asked to stand aside.

Certainly majorities have sometimes been shown to have failed to consider minority viewpoints. As a card-carrying member of the classics establishment, had I too failed to consider an interesting and possibly valid minority point of view? I could see why Keohane did not want to take sides. No one can fight every battle, and no one was being hurt or injured in this volley of words. In any case, it was only too easy to think that there was nothing urgent about mere ancient history questions. It was all so long ago. No ancient person was likely to rise up from the dead and cause trouble.

Inadvertently, I had done a lot that allowed her to suppose that I was involved in some sort of personal quarrel with Tony Martin. Hadn't I tried to change the text of his course description? Hadn't I asked if I could speak to the black students' society?

I had known Nan Keohane from her student days as one of the most intelligent and capable of all Wellesley graduates. Surely Keohane knew that the rhetoric of the student letter was overwrought. Here was a perfect opportunity to convene a discussion group or even a task force to explore the issues that were being debated. A constructive resolution was possible: Ask instructors to make their students aware of the theory of the Stolen Legacy and speak about its meaning as a myth; at the same time, ask everyone to make their students aware of the documented origins of Greek philosophy. I have in fact been doing just that since 1992.

Had Keohane or Marshall encouraged further discussion, we might have been able to address and to avoid some of the problems that later reemerged in much more sinister forms. As it was, the extreme resentment expressed in the students' letter was allowed to fester, and issues of serious educational importance were swept under the rug. All of us, but most especially our students, would have been able to learn something from the debate. From an educational point of view, silence and "moving on" is not always the right response.

It would have been a perfect moment to insist that the discussion be conducted with civility. Etiquette is not simply a set of rules about pouring tea or wearing white gloves. It is concerned with community harmony.[12] Like the law, it has a serious if unrecognized ethical function. It encourages people to show respect for others who may disagree with them. The normal rules of reasoned discourse aren't tools of the oppressor. They're time-tested techniques of making progress and coming to new levels of mutual understanding, in the interests of preventing social discord. Etiquette does not deny the right to absolute freedom of speech, but it asks for a measure of voluntary self-restraint.

Dean Marshall hoped that the faculty seminar on Bernal's work would encourage a dialogue. Eighteen colleagues from a diverse range of disciplines applied to participate, and despite our differences we did learn something from each other. Some of us even met a few times early the following fall to continue the discussion. Tony Martin hadn't applied, but I had written to him urging him to do so. Eventually he said he was willing to come, but he spoke up only once, to say that the notion that whites and blacks might be able to work together was "childish." He commented later in an interview: "We never really got to engage in a debate. . . . It just didn't happen."[13]

Well, that might also have been because he only bothered to attend four out of the nine meetings.

CHAPTER FOUR

Turning Myths
into History

I n the ancient world, myths retained their emotive and imaginative power long after people ceased to believe in the literal existence of the traditional gods. Myths coexist alongside of, and despite, philosophy and science, because they offer an immediately accessible, emotional means of understanding forces beyond human control. The idea of a Stolen Legacy expresses deep human resentment against Europeans who had stolen people from Africa and exploited its manpower and natural resources during colonization. Did European exploitation begin in antiquity? Might Western civilization, including the ancient Greek culture that had long been regarded as its foundation, have its roots in Africa? It would be satisfying to some people if this were true. But it simply was not.

Another myth that addresses the same issues was the story of the black scientist Yakub, who invented a white race of devils to plague and test black men. The Yakub myth may have been invented by W. D. Fard, the founder of the Black Muslim Temple of Islam, which was the forerunner of the Nation of Islam.[1]

Stories such as these, I was discovering, were being used to challenge what more and more people were asserting to be the Eurocentrism of university curricula. In a 1991 book, *Behind the Eurocentric Veils,* Clinton Jean argued that the exploitative mentality of Europeans had caused the evils of the twentieth century.[2] He believed that Marxism offered greater hope for mankind than capitalism, but that it too was flawed. Instead he proposed an Afrocentric alternative.

According to Jean, Africans produced the first civilizations; ancient Egypt was an African civilization, and ancient Egyptian culture was superior to the more materialistic ancient Greek culture. African culture, Jean says, was generally more civilized than European, which was more militaristic; it was matrilineal, not patriarchal like Greece and Rome. The Greeks who ruled Egypt after the conquest of Alexander transformed the benign and accessible government of the pharaohs into a soulless, hierarchical, and controlling state. Revising historical thinking, Jean argued, would elevate blackness, and that, in the long run, would be good not only for blacks but for everybody.[3]

Jean's revision of history was in fact a kind of noble lie, like the myth that Plato had devised to explain the rigid social stratification imposed in his ideal Republic.[4] Could it really be argued that Africans were less warlike than other peoples? Could one talk about Africa and Europe as if they were single entities when each was made up of many different ethnic groups speaking many different languages? Could ancient Egyptian culture be considered synonymous with ancient cultures in West Africa about which, in ancient times, little or nothing was known? The main fact we do have about the ancient world is that Egypt was separated from West Africa by the Sahara, which would indicate that their cultures would have developed more or less in isolation. And in judging Jean's ideas, one had to reflect that the only unifying feature in his notion of a specifically European or African "culture" seemed to be skin color.

The other surprising feature of Jean's explanation of the past was his assessment of the role played by Jews in fostering the integration of blacks in the United States.[5] In his view, Jews had indeed successfully communicated the needs and culture of blacks to other whites, but because Jews continued to separate themselves from blacks, their dominance in the civil rights movement itself could be regarded as a form of racism.

This attitude did not take account of the sincerely altruistic motives of Jews who had supported black organizations, and risked and even gave their lives to end segregation in the American South.[6] Perhaps for some Jews there was some self-interest involved, because they too would stand to benefit from an end to discrimination.[7]

This whole vision of the past was, in short, a new myth in the making. As a longtime student and teacher of ancient mythologies, I was fascinated to realize that what I was witnessing was a myth in the process of creation—the Jewish exploitation of blacks. At the same time it was also unsettling to realize that, as a Jew, I was one of its targets. The central text of this mythology is

The Secret Relationship Between Blacks and Jews, an anonymously authored work published in 1991 by the Nation of Islam.[8]

The principal contention of *The Secret Relationship* is that Jews were responsible for funding the African slave trade. Most previous studies of the slave trade attribute only a small role to Jews, who at the time were a mere 2 percent of the total population of the United States. *The Secret Relationship*'s anonymous authors drew almost exclusively on the work of Jewish writers to support their claims. This was said to make their propositions more credible. The book is 334 pages long. It appears to be carefully documented, with copious citations and some 1,275 footnotes (which are very easy to count, because they are numbered successively instead of starting anew with each chapter, as most books do). The cumulative numbering seemed calculated to reassure readers that it had been carefully researched.

The introduction of *The Secret Relationship* reminds its readers that although Jews have "faced blanket expulsion" more frequently than any other people in the world, they "have been conclusively linked to the greatest criminal endeavor ever undertaken against an entire race of people—a crime against humanity—the Black African Holocaust."[9] *The Secret Relationship* alleged that the Jews, themselves the victims of a Holocaust, were in fact perpetrators of the kind of crimes from which they in turn suffered at the hands of the Nazis. *The Secret Relationship* also charged Jews with secretly acknowledging this truth while denying it to the public.

Now I saw why the students who wrote the letter to the *Wellesley News* made a special point of mentioning that a *New York Times* writer with a German name was "Jewish." If he was

Jewish, and he was willing to say that the pharaohs from Nubia were black, perhaps they supposed it was more likely that Jews like me would be prepared to believe him. Or was the point rather that some Jews knew the truth, even though others obviously didn't? Citations in *The Secret Relationship* had been doctored to show that even Jewish writers seemed willing to acknowledge the awful truth about Jewish domination of the slave trade.

Any fair-minded reader can see that *The Secret Relationship* is not a work of scholarship. Rather, as Harold Brackman has shown in a careful study, it is "an anti-Semitic polemic masquerading as history."[10] Large sections of it were inspired by Henry Ford's *The International Jew: The World's Foremost Problem*, which was published in the 1920s along with a reissue of *The Protocols of the Elders of Zion*.[11] The *Protocols*, although still widely circulated around the world, are themselves a forgery, based on a political satire published in 1864 against Napoleon III by a French lawyer. Originally they had nothing to do with Jews at all, and of course there is not and never has been an international organization of Jewish Elders. Ford hated Jews for their liberalism, and indeed, for their support of "Negroes" and "Negro welfare society."[12]

The authors of *The Secret Relationship* continually misquote Jewish sources, taking quotations out of context, or citing as support works that actually say the opposite of what they are claiming.[13] They make a number of claims that are impossible to substantiate, such as that Jews (rather than Arabs) dominated the transatlantic slave trade; that they were the dominant slave traders and holders in the South; that they raped black women; that they infected Native Americans with smallpox (the "proof" of this last claim being that Sir Jeffrey Amherst bought blankets from a Jewish merchant); that Jews during the Civil War cared more about profits than about patriotism.[14]

The known facts about the slave trade give a completely different picture of the level of Jewish participation. In Europe most Jews were confined to ghettos and living in poverty. In this country, only one or two Jews were slave traders.[15] Although relatively few Jews owned slaves, Jews with property did not own large plantations, but tended to live in cities. In the towns where they lived, they tended to own fewer slaves than their Christian neighbors.[16] Although Jews may not have played a significant role, the claim that the slave trade was a "holocaust" seems to be justified.[17] Estimates by responsible historians indicate that perhaps as many as eleven million people from Africa were sold into slavery, of whom as many as a million may have died in transit.[18] Only about 300,000 were brought to North America.

Why did the Nation of Islam take such trouble to create a revised or alternative "history" of the slave trade? One reason, certainly, was to keep people's attention away from the slave trading that continued long after the outcome of the American Civil War put a stop to the transatlantic slave trade. The traders in this case were not Europeans or Jews but Arabs, and this is a bit of an embarrassment for an organization that calls itself the Nation of Islam. That slave trade is still continuing at present in Sudan.[19] The U.S. State Department, at least, was well aware of its existence during the 1990s and after. Louis Farrakhan, the leader of the Nation of Islam, said nothing about it, although he must have known that it was going on, since he had visited Sudan in 1994.

Of course, the other reason for accusing Jews of being

responsible for the slave trade was to rekindle and intensify existing anti-Semitism. Some attention had already been given to anti-Semitic eruptions around the United States, because of a hair-raising speech that Leonard Jeffries gave in the summer of 1991 at the Empire State Black Arts and Cultural Festival in Albany that raised a storm of controversy.[20] The *New York Post* had published an account of it. Jeffries was then head of the Black Studies Department at the City College of New York. He claimed that Jews had played a major role in the slave trade. He also claimed that Russian Jews were in league with the Mafia, and that Jews, through their domination of the Hollywood film industry, encouraged the hatred of blacks. He singled out Diane Ravitch, then assistant U.S. secretary for education, as a "Jew" and a "racist."

In the summer of 1992, Henry Louis Gates, Jr., chairman of African-American Studies at Harvard, wrote an op-ed essay for the *New York Times* about *The Secret Relationship* and its anti-Semitic allegations.[21] He observed that anti-Semitism was on the rise in black communities. In his opinion, this new anti-Semitism was "engineered and promoted by leaders who affect to be speaking for a larger resentment." This movement's bible was *The Secret Relationship,* and the book's conclusions were "increasingly treated as damning historical fact." Gates informed his readers about some of the book's most glaring misrepresentations, and he warned that the book was only the first volume in a promised series.

Gates also described how the new anti-Semitism played out in everyday encounters between blacks and Jews. Blacks now demanded apologies from Jews for the slave trade and other injustices.

Some wanted more than an apology; they sought reparations.[22] It was easy enough simply to plug into existing anti-Semitism. Above all, leaders like Farrakhan wanted to separate blacks from Jews, indeed from all other people, because they believed that blacks would have more power in isolation. Gates, following Martin Luther King, thought that was just what blacks should *not* be doing: "'Whatever affects one directly affects us all indirectly.' How easy to forget this—and how vital to remember."

For a few months I thought, or rather hoped, that this new anti-Semitism would never manifest itself at Wellesley. Perhaps a few of us were being oversensitive in reading meaning into the gratuitous references to Jewish ethnicity in the students' letter to the college paper. Or when we wondered why Tony Martin had gone out of his way to remark in the Africana Studies Department newsletter that his Africans in Antiquity course had "come under attack from a Jewish Studies specialist in the Religion department" when he first proposed it to the faculty in 1978.[23]

Of course the anti-Semitism had been there all along. In February 1993, according to an article in the college paper, some students discovered that the notorious *Secret Relationship Between Blacks and Jews* was on the reading list of Tony Martin's Africana Studies course Introduction to African American History, 1500 to the Present.[24] A student went to talk with him about the book during the professor's office hours, but he refused to meet with her. Martin later admitted that he was reluctant to meet with students "on an individual basis," but would consider a group discussion. He asked why no one had raised a question about his use of the book during his first-semester course The Internationalization of Black Power. He observed: "I consider this an intolerable situation in an academic environment such as this. If these Jews really want to see racist material in the classroom, then let them stop any African-American student on campus."[25] Presumably he meant that white racism was so endemic in the rest of the Wellesley curriculum that every black student on campus would have just cause for complaint about what he or she had been asked to study in other courses.

I was quoted in the article, but in fact I hadn't known about the students' complaint concerning Martin's use of this book until the reporter who interviewed me told me about it. President Keohane and Nancy Kolodny, who had replaced Dale Marshall as dean of the college, were also interviewed. They spoke in vague terms about the importance of informed discussion. Kolodny "emphasized the rights of professors to exercise their academic freedom."[26] Later, in a meeting, the faculty present affirmed the right of any professor to use any book, as well as the fact that academic freedom guarantees that faculty members who disapprove of a particular book or approach have a right to say so—in other words, that controversial issues should be discussed.

This new willingness on the part of the administration to begin to talk about the issues was at least progress from the ostrich-like avoidance they had practiced in the past. It helped that the intellectual issues were more clear-cut than in the case of the alleged theft of Greek philosophy. Most people were prepared to acknowledge that anti-Semitism was a form of racism. And most could see that *The Secret Relationship* was hate literature masquerading as a serious book. It also helped that the people being attacked (Jews) were a living constituency, who could speak out for themselves, and who were a powerful group among the alumnae. After all, the most sensitive region of an academic administration's anatomy is its institutional pocketbook.

Nonetheless, I continued to feel that the discussion of academic freedom still did not go far enough. As faculty we were concerned to safeguard our own privileges and freedom from interference. But at some point the rights of students also needed to be considered: weren't our students entitled in their courses to the best and most accurate information that we could offer them? What were we doing to ensure that *that* was happening? The answer, of course, was not very much—and not just at Wellesley but many other places in the country. If the quality of a Wellesley education was generally excellent, it was only because most of the faculty held themselves to the highest standards as individuals. Institutional oversight had almost nothing to do with it.

It was a difficult year for me, not just because of all this controversy. In July 1992 I discovered that I had breast cancer, and during most of the following academic year I was undergoing chemotherapy. I was teaching only half-time, and my energy was limited and ever declining as the course of treatment went on. But the frightening illness gave me an opportunity to reflect on priorities, and to read and think. I was determined, if I survived, to discover the origin of the myth of the Stolen Legacy, and to keep on speaking and writing about it.

In February 1993 I had a chance to follow up on my resolutions. The speaker at the annual Martin Luther King lecture turned out to be none other than the famous Afrocentric writer Dr. Yosef A. A. ben-Jochannan, author of *Africa: The Mother of Western Civilization,* in which he claims that Aristotle stole his philosophy from the library at Alexandria.

By this time I knew what "Dr. Ben" was likely to say. But I was shocked to hear Nan Keohane introduce him as a "distinguished Egyptologist." Keohane had read my *New Republic* article. Did she really believe that she was going to hear a lecture on Egyptology? What ben-Jochannan delivered, without notes, like a sermon, was a rundown of the Stolen Legacy theory.

Originally the Martin Luther King lecture had been an all-college event designed to bring the community together. Now it seemed to have become just the opposite.[27] On this occasion, there were only about twenty-five to thirty students there, virtually all of them African-American, and only a few members of the faculty and administration were present. Some of them, I knew, had read my article and had been following the "debate," such as it was. But after the lecture was over, no one seemed prepared to raise a question about what ben-Jochannan had been saying. So I raised my hand, and when called on I asked: "Sir, you said that Aristotle stole his philosophy from the library at Alexandria, but how would that have been possible, when the library was not built until after his death?" Dr. Ben responded that the dates were uncertain.

"Rubbish," said my husband, Sir Hugh Lloyd-Jones, quite audibly. He is a famous classical scholar, and he knew that there was no question about the date of Aristotle's death (322 B.C.) and also that there was no possibility the library could have existed until some years after the city of Alexandria had been planned and settlers had arrived to build it, around 297 B.C. British scholars are accustomed to voicing criticism openly. But in the context of this particular lecture, the remark (however true) was offensive and tactless. It provided a perfect opening for ben-Jochannan to avoid giving an answer by taking umbrage instead. He said, "I resent the tone of the question." A student who was doing honors work with Tony Martin stood up and apologized to the speaker for our rudeness and pointedly walked out, her high heels clattering across the stage.

President Keohane had left after the lecture itself and hadn't heard the discussion. If she had stayed on, she would have heard ben-Jochannan give the students some troubling advice. He told them to go along with whatever their instructors told them in class, even when they did not believe it, in order to get a good grade. But they could and should believe what *black* instructors told them, and should in particular entrust themselves to "Dr. Tony."[28] He observed that although they might think that Jews were all "hook-nosed and sallow-faced," there were other Jews who looked like himself (he is a Falasha or Ethiopian Jew).

After the talk my husband and I were surrounded by students, some angry, others willing to listen. I tried to explain that I had learned from my graduate training to look at evidence. "You were *trained,* all right," said one young man, obviously not a Wellesley student. More politely, other students insisted that although my husband and I thought we knew the truth, "He is telling the truth. What you learned is wrong."

I now realized that although the Martin Luther King lecture was officially open to the public, in practice it had become a kind of youth rally or indoctrination session. Real discussion and debate weren't welcome. How could that be possible, let alone tolerable, in an academic institution? And how was it possible not to be disturbed by what Dr. ben-Jochannan had been telling these students about the ancient Greeks? I couldn't sleep all night thinking about it.

I decided to post a brief message to an online chat group about the classics, outlining the gist of the ben-Jochannan lecture and the dangers posed to our subject by the Stolen Legacy theory. The message did not mention Tony Martin or the controversy on our campus. Nonetheless, after someone at Franklin and Marshall College had forwarded a copy of the message to him, Martin distributed copies of it during a meeting of the Wellesley student senate.[29] The meeting was a forum titled "How We Speak to One Another," intended to address the controversy surrounding his use of *The Secret Relationship Between Blacks and Jews.* Martin observed that the "e-mail message is a prime example of slander at this college. In addition, the historical conflict between blacks and Jews is long, but there are more people outside of these communities who are interested in the conflict persisting."

One student senator at the meeting said: "People have put Professor Martin on trial. This seems to happen to him a lot, especially by Professor Lefkowitz." Another said, "The person who wrote this e-mail message had attacked the professor and his department many times before." Others pointed out that my e-mail was not relevant to the discussion, and asked, somewhat tendentiously, whether Martin had obtained my permission to copy it. Unfortunately, no one had the courage to ask why Tony Martin thought my objections to the Stolen Legacy theory or to ben-Jochannan's anti-Semitism amounted to an attack upon himself, or why he sought to defend himself not on substance but by playing the race card.

At the next meeting of the Academic Council, Martin made a formal statement of his concerns. The members of the Academic Council consist of the entire faculty and selected administrators.

Certain representatives of the student government and the college newspaper are invited to attend as auditors. More students than usual attended this particular meeting (on March 4, 1993), although technically it was not open to anyone other than its designated members. The controversy about *The Secret Relationship* was on the docket, and Martin went to the microphone to deliver a prepared speech.[30]

Until Martin gave his defining speech, it might have been possible to suppose that he was primarily using *The Secret Relationship Between Blacks and Jews* as an *illustration* of the new anti-Semitism. But to the horror of the audience, or, I hoped, most of them, he made it clear from the start that he enthusiastically approved of it: "*The Secret Relationship Between Blacks and Jews* . . . is an excellent study of Jewish involvement in the transatlantic slave trade and African slavery." Martin made a point of giving numerous examples from the "primarily Jewish sources" used in the book. Jews regarded the book as anti-Semitic because they were opposed to the Black Power movement, which was run by blacks. Jews in the twentieth century had supported black causes only as long as they served to promote their own "self-interest." He rejected out of hand the work of "the Jewish scholar Nathan Glazer," who had argued that Jews had not been particularly supportive of segregation in the South.

He then listed all that I had done to criticize his work, accusing me of having "insulted" ben-Jochannan and of "intriguing" with the dean of the college to change his course description. He claimed that I had attacked his Africans in Antiquity course in "the conservative Jewish-owned *New Republic*." He noted that "Hillel" students had sat in on his course "in order to monitor" his references to *The Secret Relationship*. Although Professor Glazer of Harvard had argued that "compensation for the past is a dangerous principle," the Germans had paid reparations to "the Jewish state of Israel." Martin concluded: "The day of Africa's reparations must come." The large group of students sitting in the back of the room applauded enthusiastically.

Here was the specific agenda that Henry Louis Gates had described in his op-ed in the *New York Times* in July 1992 as becoming increasingly prevalent: Jews are responsible for the slave trade; Jews controlled black organizations in this country; therefore Jews should pay blacks reparations.[31] Many people present were visibly stunned by the speech but did not know what to say. Others seemed not to grasp what was going on. One member of the faculty (who was not an American historian) even congratulated Martin for taking a brave and unconventional stance in arguing that Jews were responsible for the slave trade!

I defended myself as best I could against Martin's charges, as I had done repeatedly in the past.[32] I said that I was only trying to address issues of fact and interpretation in history. I pointed out that I had been asked to write for the *New Republic* and the *Chronicle of Higher Education* and the *New York Times* not because I was Jewish, but because I was an authority in my field. In the context of the present discussion I thought that needed to be said, even though it ought to have gone without saying.

After the meeting a colleague approached me. He was visibly angry at me. He had been active in the college's Committee on Racism, and it was now evident that much of his painstaking work had been in vain. I said: "But Tony [Martin] is teaching people that Aristotle stole his philosophy from the library at

Alexandria!" He replied sternly: "I don't care who stole what from whom." I understood my irate colleague to mean that ancient history was unimportant, that I was to be blamed for disrupting campus harmony, and that my concerns about what was going on in Tony Martin's classroom, racial or factual, were trivial.

Perhaps he was angry not so much at me as at the meeting. He, like most of the rest of us, had assumed that we had been making progress, and that tough issues could be resolved through patience and understanding, and that blacks and whites could coexist in harmony, side-by-side. The meeting simply revealed what all of us had been trying hard to ignore for too long. He was upset with me for bringing all the unpleasantness finally to light. Hatred was indeed being taught, in and out of the classroom. Anti-Semitism was involved. One could maintain that alternative nonfactual histories were acceptable, but not teaching hatred of a living people.

Moreover, so long as anti-Semitic ideas were being taught, even to a few students, no easy resolution was possible. We had been deluding ourselves with the myth that education, along with good will, had healed all rifts in our society. We had forgotten that education and reason do not have the instant appeal that hatred and anger can supply. Since academics were not accustomed to dealing with violent emotions, and because we generally lacked the vocabulary to respond to them effectively, it felt more convenient for us to assume that hatred and anger were not present, at least, not on our campus, not *here*. If we saw evidence of them, we wanted to see them as anomalous, so that we could continue to imagine that we were making progress. We were not prepared for that most painful of all history lessons, reality.

I was still sitting in my place in the Academic Council chamber when two colleagues came up, Robin Akert in psychology and Julie Drucker in political science. They were horrified by what had happened and asked what they could do to help. I was still so shaken that I asked them to walk back with me to my office, and then to my car in the parking lot (it was now after sunset). On our way to the car we ran into Marcellus Andrews, an economics professor, who had gone to the library instead of to the meeting. As we walked along talking about what had just happened, we saw that Tony Martin was right behind us, accompanied by an attractive young woman.

Andrews pointedly escorted me to the car and got in beside me, and Akert and Drucker went back to their respective offices. After I drove Andrews to the commuter rail station, we sat in the car talking about Martin's speech. Andrews held my hand and did his best to cheer me up. Andrews is an African American who was outspoken in his criticism of Martin's writings and actions. He was later to write in the *Wellesley News* that to pretend that Jews are responsible for our modern civil rights nightmare is "stupid, criminal, or worse."[33] What could we do about "tenured racists," he asked. "We should keep them around and ridicule them without end."

At the time I was too depressed to see that Martin's speech was the best possible thing. It had finally made people aware that we indeed had a real problem, one that would not go away no matter how hard we tried not to see it. The Wellesley faculty and administration finally did come to grips with the historical issues raised by the use of *The Secret Relationship*. President Keohane wrote a letter to the *Wellesley News*, saying that controversial

Department had brought these issues to the attention of the Wellesley faculty again, with his teaching about the Holocaust in spring 1991—long after the quotas had been eliminated.[40]

But there was a distinct difference between the new activism and the old anti-Semitism, as I knew from personal experience. I had attended both the Brearley School in New York City and Wellesley itself in the 1950s, when informal Jewish quotas were in existence. WASP anti-Semitism in those days tended to be undercover, passive, and only exclusionary. I doubt if many of those who practiced it, however unthinkingly, had in mind the old libels about Jews killing Christ or desecrating the Host on Jewish holidays. If asked, they would have said that they were trying to save the majority of places in their schools for the descendants of the kind of people who founded the institutions. Jews weren't invited to certain gatherings or encouraged to pursue particular careers for similar reasons.

What the ADL was faced with now was different. It was overt and actively hostile, more like the anti-Semitic propaganda distributed by the Nazis in the 1930s than the discreet silence of the 1950s.[41] It alleged that Jews controlled the government and the media and that, in addition to being responsible for the slave trade, they were "imposter" Jews.[42] It was now claimed that Exodus, Psalms, and other books in the Bible were written by Egyptian pharaohs and that the Israelites were merely the transmitters of an older Egyptian religion. The real Jews were black, as Dr. ben-Jochannan had implied in his answer to a question after his lecture at Wellesley.[43]

Leonard Zakim, the regional director of the ADL, and the ADL's legal counsel Sally Greenberg met with Nan Keohane.[44]

Zakim believed that Martin's "Broadside" wasn't protected by the legal doctrine of academic freedom. It was not just something that was said in a classroom discussion, but an open "polemic against the Jewish community," published outside the context of the classroom.

Martin Goldman, the associate director of the American Jewish Committee (AJC), agreed that a joint statement ought to be made by all four local Jewish advocacy groups.[45] As it happened, Goldman was familiar with racial politics in the academic world. He had done graduate work in black studies but could not get a tenure-track job because he was white. He had some years before been interviewed by Wellesley, but (as it happened) the position had been given to Tony Martin. By his own account, Goldman's knowledge of the Wellesley scene contributed to his determination to *do something* rather than simply request that college officials address the issue of anti-Semitism in whatever ways they thought best.[46]

Goldman took the lead in getting the Jewish advocacy groups to issue a joint statement that "called upon the Trustees and administration of Wellesley to review the behavior and status of Martin."[47] Or, as Goldman summarized the statement for the college newspaper, "We are asking the College to look at what he's written in the newsletter to see if anti-Semitic ideas exceed the bounds of what is a legitimate point of view . . . and if so, whether Martin should be kept on in the community of scholars."

The statement did not demand that Martin be dismissed. But a request from outside the college that a professor's status be reviewed because of what he had said was an invasion of academic freedom. Most academics, including me, would have spoken out in Martin's defense. What protects one of us protects us all. Tenure, with all its obvious faults, is the only certain means of ensuring that a faculty member can speak out about controversial issues. Without it, any influential group could put pressure on individual faculty members to promote a particular agenda, whether it be Christian doctrine, intelligent design, Holocaust denial, political correctness, or indeed, as in this case, anti-Semitism. Without it I would have never been free to speak up about the Stolen Legacy theory.

The Jewish advocacy groups believed that they could make a valid distinction between freedom to speak out in the classroom and freedom to write outside the classroom. But in practice such distinctions are almost impossible to make. In the case of Michael Levin, a professor whose research findings had been considered racist by some members of the administration and faculty at the City College of New York, the courts found in 1991 and 1992 that academic freedom extended also to publications.[48]

The Jewish organizations might have been on stronger ground had they asked the college to consider whether or not *hate speech* was protected by academic freedom. That question has acquired new relevance in the wake of attacks on civilians instigated by Muslim terrorists. In such cases intervention would be appropriate. But Martin, to the best of anyone's knowledge, had never advocated the use of physical violence in his "Broadside" or indeed anything else he had written. All he was asking for was the payment of reparations. The college, quite rightly, did not review Martin's tenure.

CHAPTER FIVE

A New Anti-Semitism

Although the Jewish organizations' joint statement failed to persuade the college to take any kind of action against Tony Martin, it did have one significant consequence. It became the principal justification for the publication of Martin's notorious book *The Jewish Onslaught: Despatches from the Wellesley Battlefront.*[1] The first sentence on the back cover reads: "The Jewish attack on Black progress reached Wellesley College in 1993, when more Jewish organizations than you could shake a stick at issued a call for the dismissal of Dr. Tony Martin from his tenured professorship at the elite women's college." That sounded a lot more ominous than it was. Only four Jewish organizations were involved: the ADL, the AJC, the American Jewish Congress, and the Jewish Community Relations Council.

It was, to say the least, unusual for a group of Jewish organizations to work together so closely. But their cooperation could now be seen as evidence for a Jewish conspiracy. Martin once again used the rhetoric of war: "I am under siege . . . I do feel I am being unfairly attacked."[2] *The Jewish Onslaught* was advertised in the spring 1993 issue of the Nation of Islam's *Blacks and Jews News*. It was offered at a reduced rate in the autumn 1993 issue if purchased along with *The Secret Relationship*.[3]

I knew that *The Jewish Onslaught* was going to be published later in the year because I had been a subscriber (under an assumed name) to the Nation of Islam's *Blacks and Jews News* ever since I bought my copy of *The Secret Relationship* from their Boston office in 1992. When I told a senior member of the Wellesley administration that Martin was going to publish the book, she exclaimed: "Oh, come on, that simply isn't going to happen!" Did she suppose I was making it up because I had good reason to disapprove of what its author had been saying? Or (more likely) did she assume that such a thing simply could not happen at a place like Wellesley?

Martin began distributing copies of *The Jewish Onslaught* at the reception after an all-college lecture by Princeton professor Cornel West, in late November 1993. West had been invited because he was known to have been eager to establish a dialogue between blacks and Jews.

There are some eighty pages of text in Martin's book. The rest of it, some fifty more pages, consists primarily of documents and letters. The book was published by Tony Martin's own firm The Majority Press, also known as the TM Press, a publishing house that specializes in his own works and those of other West

Indian authors (Martin himself hails from Trinidad). Certainly no major trade publisher or university press would have been prepared to consider such a manuscript.

As an editorial writer for the *Boston Globe* observed, "the book is an almost hysterical string of examples, from centuries-old talmudic ideas to the presence of Jewish newscasters such as Ted Koppel, Mike Wallace and Barbara Walters as proof of Jewish oppression."[4] The hero of the story was Martin himself, confronting the evil monolithic enemy (the Jews), with their obedient servants, the "good Negroes," such as Wellesley's Selwyn Cudjoe, who had condemned Martin's use of *The Secret Relationship*, and the "Black Jewish spokesman" Marcellus Andrews as well as "America's most notorious Judeophile," Henry Louis Gates, Jr.[5]

Predictably, Martin included much of the material he had already discussed in his "Broadsides," but with heightened rhetoric and a new emphasis on ethnic labeling. Martin Bernal was "the white Jewish king of Afrocentricland," even though Bernal was "Jewish" only to the extent that his father's father was a Spanish Sephardic Jew who had settled in Ireland and had become a Roman Catholic.[6] One couldn't help being reminded of the Nazi era, when people were considered Jewish if they had Jewish antecedents, even if they had adopted Christianity.

Martin did everything he could to characterize Martin Bernal as an ally of mine and an enemy of Afrocentrism. Bernal was in fact "touting a hypothesis for a Jewish origin of Greek civilization." "If Lefkowitz has her way, one will be able to find few Africans in Africa, for all the Jews she places there. She sees the Carthaginians and Phoenicians as somehow Jewish," Martin wrote.[7] I was "well known as a national leader of the Jewish onslaught against Afrocentrism in general and me [Martin] in particular."[8]

More interesting still, at least to connoisseurs of hate literature, was Martin's methodology. Like the anonymous authors of *The Secret Relationship,* he used Jewish sources to document his allegations against Jews, presumably because that would make his assertions more credible, as when he alleged that he could not receive fair treatment by the media, on the grounds that they were mostly owned by Jews.[9] Had he been inspired by *The Secret Relationship*? Was he even involved with the book's authors, the Historical Research Committee of the Nation of Islam? It wasn't unthinkable, especially given his outspoken appreciation of their work.

Like *The Secret Relationship, The Jewish Onslaught* advocates openly for Jews to pay reparations to blacks. The relationship between the groups, Martin argues, must now be new and "more mutually dignified."[10] The old alliance between the two groups, in which the Jews played a dominant role, would have to be abandoned. Dialogue was needed (meaning that Jews needed to listen to blacks); then apologies (by Jews to blacks); then *reparations.*

In many ways, the publication of this book made it easier for Wellesley's administration and faculty to distance themselves from Martin. A few days after *The Jewish Onslaught* was published, our new president, Diana Chapman Walsh (Nan Keohane had left to become president of Duke University) sent a letter to everyone in the college community and to all the alumnae of the college about the book.[11] She reaffirmed Martin's right to express himself freely, without fear of reprisal. At the same time, she said that it was necessary to speak out against the book, because it violated the basic values of the community and of academic discourse:

> Rhetoric of this kind undermines the force and critical exchange of ideas on which teaching and scholarship rest. Professor Martin's book crosses the line from simply unpopular or controversial argument to unnecessarily disrespectful and deeply divisive speech that must be countered, however strong the temptation not to dignify it with a response.

Walsh's letter took the discussion to a new and more productive level. She made a distinction between controversial speech and hate speech, and she also pointed out that certain norms of civility needed to be observed in order to promote a productive exchange of ideas. Her prompt action encouraged others to begin to ask hard questions about appropriate course content and the limits of academic freedom.

Faculty members also were prepared to speak out. At a meeting of the Academic Council on December 16, 1993, non-Jewish members of the faculty expressed their concerns about *The Jewish Onslaught*. Two spoke about the divisive effects of hate speech on all members of the community. William Cain of the English Department questioned the quality of the readings Martin had chosen for his Introduction to African American History course. Why was Martin assigning unchallenging works written on a high-school level? Why weren't some of the major works in the field included? Why had the quality of Martin's own writings fallen off from the high standard he had set for himself earlier in his career? As a specialist in American literature, with a long-standing interest in African-American works, Cain was well qualified to ask these questions.

The next day Cain described Martin's response to his remarks in a message posted on the public electronic bulletin board, which was open to everyone in the college capable of using e-mail:

> After Council ended, Professor Martin walked over to me and delivered an attack filled with four-letter words. Others were present nearby and heard him. He could have approached me and argued forcefully for his choice of books; he could have tried to explain and justify those choices and therefore make the case that I was wrong. Instead, Professor Martin settled for the easy way of curses and name-calling.[12]

Martin's reaction, Cain explained, unpleasant as it had been to listen to, did at least explain why so far it had been impossible to discuss the issues with him: "All criticism is turned into demonization and thus is left unanswered." Certainly Cain's remarks about Martin's scholarship were uncomfortably direct and to the point, but Cain was justified in observing that in an academic context Martin's response was inappropriate.

Questions about academic quality needed to be raised if we were ever to begin to confront the *academic* issues raised by Martin's praise of the scholarship in *The Secret Relationship*. How could someone who thought of himself as a historian think that *The Secret Relationship* was an "excellent study"? How could anyone who was prepared to look at the evidence believe that *Jews* were primarily responsible for the slave trade? There were also

A few years later, in their book about suppression of academic freedom on American campuses, Alan Charles Kors and Harvey Silverglate suggested that Martin's academic freedom might have been infringed by Walsh's letter.[18] But they appear to have supposed that in her capacity as president Walsh had the power to control the status and salary of individual faculty members. At Wellesley, promotion and merit increases are determined not by the president alone but on the advice of an elected faculty committee. So in retrospect there is no reason to doubt that Walsh did the right thing. She made it clear that although faculty can say and teach what they want they must also bear responsibility for their words and actions. Once again an imprecise discussion of a general principle like "academic freedom" had been used to fog the issue. Martin's rights and his academic freedoms had never been put at risk by anyone at Wellesley.

Some faculty members were willing to join Walsh in speaking out. In February 1994, Guy Rogers in the History Department and Jonathan Imber in Sociology circulated a petition that was signed by more than half the faculty (most of them tenured), decrying the *ad hominem* attacks and anti-Semitism in *The Jewish Onslaught*.[19] Where, I wondered, were the other half of the faculty? Most of the untenured faculty, unsurprisingly, also abstained. Perhaps some were nervous about making a judgment outside their own fields. Perhaps some were indifferent, or frightened of taking a side in the controversy that might make them vulnerable to a charge of racism for criticizing a black person. Martin was certainly not being singled out because he was black; Walsh surely would have mounted the same criticism had he been white.[20] Perhaps, in a country where only a fraction of eligible voters bother to come to the polls, the best one can hope for is partial engagement.

In the end the History Department found an effective way to address the academic issues in the case. They voted *not* to count toward a history major any courses in the Africana Studies Department. The courses that had previously received credit were all taught by Martin. Jonathan Knudsen, the chairman of the History Department, observed:

> The way [Martin] reasons, the way he analyses historical material, the view of history maintained in the book—basically a conspiracy theory—were inconsistent with those of a professional historian and incompatible with our own view of pedagogy in history.[21]

Some members of the faculty objected to this decision, largely citing Martin's academic freedom.[22] But no one had stopped him from teaching the course in the Africana Studies Department, or prevented students taking his courses from receiving credit for them toward an Africana Studies major.

In late spring 1994, President Walsh, following the recommendation of the Committee on Faculty Appointments, told Martin that he had not been granted a merit increase to his salary.[23] She cited in her letter to him "the recent degradation of your scholarship and the apparent effects on the quality of your teaching." Martin believed that the action had been taken in requital for his writing *The Jewish Onslaught*. Because that in his view was an infringement of his right to freedom of speech, he threatened to sue the college, as he had done a decade before when Nan Keohane was president.

In the end, the very fact that Martin had written and had no regrets about a book called *The Jewish Onslaught* had lost him the support of most of the faculty colleagues who had been willing to give him the benefit of the doubt, and who still clung to the hope that he didn't really mean what he said in his speech about *The Secret Relationship* and my collusion with the Jewish media. Ironically, at least from his point of view, Martin's own words and actions did more to discredit him and his cause than anything the Jewish organizations had said or done, or anything I or anyone else had said or written.

But Martin may have considered that while he had little to lose in the way of support at Wellesley, *The Jewish Onslaught* would put him on the lecture circuit along with Leonard Jeffries, who was by this time well known for his anti-Semitic speeches, and the Nation of Islam's Khallid Muhammad, whose incendiary remarks had drawn nationwide attention when he spoke in November 1993 at Kean College in New Jersey.[24] Martin's book was reviewed with effusive enthusiasm in the autumn 1993 Nation of Islam newsletter: "*The Jewish Onslaught* is an amazing and unprecedented book. In it the scholar activist is seen at his most brilliant."[25] For some time it was one of the top ten books sold in the Los Angeles black community.[26]

Even at universities, audiences seemed eager to attend anti-Semitic rallies. In April 1994, Howard University administrators postponed a lecture on the slave trade by David Brion Davis, Sterling Professor of History at Yale and a convert to Judaism, because they were afraid he would be harassed and heckled on campus.[27] A week later Martin was one of the featured speakers at the notorious Howard University "hate-fest," a series of lectures about the "Black Holocaust." Since the event was televised on C-Span, many people had an opportunity to witness the thunderous applause, shouting, and excitement that greeted complaints about Jewish control over the Federal Reserve Bank, the media, and Hollywood, et cetera. In his lecture Martin acknowledged that Arabs and Christians were involved in the slave trade, but he placed particular emphasis on the role played by Jews. He alleged that the Babylonian Talmud was the source of the belief that blacks were inferior to whites.[28] Jews, he said, were the only people who denied "their involvement in the slave trade." "Sometimes I believe that they are totally incapable of telling the truth."[29]

In December 1994 Martin gave a lecture at the University of Massachusetts at Amherst. Before being admitted to the auditorium, everyone had to pass through a metal detector, and Martin was accompanied by five Fruit of Islam bodyguards in their signature suits, white shirts, and bow ties. Apparently they were there to make a great show of protecting Martin from the threat of physical violence from Jews. Even more absurdly, Martin later showed up with Fruit of Islam guards at a Wellesley lecture by UMass Amherst professor Julius Lester, an African American who has converted to Judaism. According to Raymond Winbush, then director of the Race Relations Institute at Fisk University, Martin went so far as to have a special ignition system installed in his car, so he could start it by remote control in case a bomb had been placed in it.[30]

But however unnecessary in reality, such theatrical precautions helped to heighten latent tension in the lecture halls where Martin spoke. At UMass Amherst Martin's topic was "Black leaders under siege." "In the current situation, you know," he said, "we once more find a Jewish onslaught right into the fore." He spoke of "incredible revelations concerning the spying of the Anti-Defamation League," and "Jewish editorial and op-ed writers who have been at the forefront of the struggle against black leadership."[31] Some black students evidently believed that Martin was telling them the truth and that there was nothing anti-Semitic about his lecture.[32] Robert Costrell, a professor of economics at UMass, was in the audience. He recalled: "[Martin] was well-received by the black students. The Jewish students were not terribly effective in Q & A. It was an ugly event."[33]

Other members of the audience were horrified not only by what they heard, but by the enthusiasm with which some of Martin's most extravagant claims were received. It wasn't just that to many young people the Holocaust was as remote as ancient history. Many of them sincerely believed that the history of black people had been systematically omitted from history books, and that they could hear the "truth" only from black professors.

These events helped to reveal some of the consequences of allowing people to construct their own narratives, without reference to the evidence. In May 1994 at Cornell University, Martin had argued that "Black people should interpret their own reality. . . . Jews have been in the forefront of efforts to thwart the interpretation of our own history."[34]

Although no one from Wellesley was around to hear it, it was in order to let Martin interpret his own view of "reality" that Dale Marshall had been willing to allow him to teach his version of ancient history, and why Martin had been so eager to avoid discussions with me. He did not want anyone to interfere with the narratives he was constructing.

CHAPTER SIX

Truth or Slander?

Socrates firmly believed that there could be no education without dialogue. He always used the technique of question and answer in his discussions, because it was essential that everyone acknowledge the validity of statements before the discussion could proceed. But at Wellesley—at least in 1993–94—what we mainly saw was confrontation.

Dialogue, at least in certain circles, had come to mean confrontation, as was implied in the closing slogan of *The Jewish Onslaught:* "Dialogue. Apologies. Reparations." Was it so certain that dialogue would result in apologies? By "dialogue," *The Jewish Onslaught* evidently meant that one side would speak, and the other side would listen.

Nothing in the discussion at Wellesley about *The Jewish*

Onslaught had managed to budge Martin an inch. In December 1993 he issued a second "Broadside," defending *The Jewish Onslaught* as a "book of analysis supported by normal scholarly documentation." Jews, he argued, have written many books on black-Jewish relations, while only two such books had been written by blacks. Why, he asked, did Jews "enjoy monopolistic privileges over a debate that concerns Blacks as well as Jews"?

Curiously, Martin now chose to complain about President Walsh's "lack of civility." Another breach of etiquette had been committed by economics professor Marcellus Andrews, who had called Martin "a racist Pied Piper." But the worst offender, he claimed, was me. In an article I had written for a newsletter called *Measure,* published in September 1993, I had, as Martin put it, "maliciously and scurrilously alleged" that he had called a student "a white fucking bitch."[1] Was Walsh, he asked in his "Broadside," aware of that? I also had said, in describing his verbal assault on Michelle Plantec: "The young woman fell down as a result of his onslaught and Martin bent over to continue his rage at her." Martin regarded this as an attack upon him, and he listed this and a number of other comments, including the "Jewish hate mail" that he had reported in *The Jewish Onslaught.*

This was not the only confrontation (or "dialogue") Martin had in mind. Although I didn't realize it at the time, what Martin wrote in this second "Broadside" was to be the basis of a lawsuit against me that he filed in December 1993. At the same time he sued two undergraduates for libel. One was Avik Roy, who had just graduated from MIT and was now at Yale Medical School. Roy was the founder of *Counterpoint,* an MIT-Wellesley student magazine that had been critical of political correctness at both insti-

tutions. Roy had written an article describing Martin's encounter
with Plantec. The passage Martin objected to was: "Counterpoint has learned that . . . Professor Martin gained tenure within
the Africana Studies Department only after successfully suing the
college for racial discrimination."[2] Martin also sued the student
publisher of *Counterpoint,* Samira Khan, and Wellesley College
for discrimination when it did not award him a merit increase.
The summons didn't reach me until late January 1994. I was in
Oxford, England, at the time, giving a lecture on the origins of
the Stolen Legacy theory. I asked my house sitter to send copies
of the summons to Nancy Kolodny, the dean of the college, and
to Martin Goldman at the American Jewish Committee.

As soon as I returned from England, just before the start
of the new semester, I went to Dean Kolodny. "It's your problem," she said. "The college can't help you. And by the way," she
added disapprovingly, "the student didn't fall down." Apparently,
Wellesley wasn't prepared to indemnify me. According to the
dean, I had not written the article in connection with my teaching or any services I had performed for the college. I might have
replied that I had written what I had because I cared about the
quality of education Wellesley students were receiving and about
anti-Semitism on our campus. But at that moment I was too depressed to come up with logical counterarguments.

Kolodny's lack of sympathy troubled me deeply. Did she
suppose that I had simply invented a description of Martin's actions out of whole cloth and that I was really guilty of malicious
libel? Some months later I learned that the college's lawyers had
advised members of the administration to dissociate themselves
from me entirely, because they thought that if Martin believed

I had the college's support, he might increase the amount he demanded in compensation for the alleged libel.

I had no idea what would happen next. So far I had been subject only to verbal abuse and allegations about my supposed motives. Now I might have to spend a lot of money simply to defend myself against a frivolous charge. I can't say that I hadn't been warned that this might happen. Some months earlier I had consulted a lawyer about whether I could sue Martin for some of the things he had been saying about me. The lawyer told me to forget it, since I hadn't really been damaged by anything Martin had said. A more serious problem, ironically, from the legal point of view, was my own vulnerability. Since I was right and he was wrong about the facts of ancient history, my having shown him to be wrong unquestionably diminished his reputation, not mine, and thus, arguably, laid a necessary predicate for any cause of action that he might bring against me.

Since my personal umbrella insurance policy with The Travelers appeared to cover libel suits, I wrote to the company, which replied that first it would need to investigate the matter, and would reply in due course. Eventually, in June 1994, the insurance company said it was prepared to take the case. The insurers chose the law firm of Donahue and Donahue in Lowell, Massachusetts, which put Michael Gallagher in charge of the case. There was no need to explain to Gallagher why I objected to the notion that Aristotle had stolen his philosophy from the library at Alexandria. Gallagher had majored in classics at Holy Cross.

But in February 1994 I urgently needed legal advice about how to deal with the summons that had been served on me. Fortunately, Martin Goldman of the American Jewish Committee knew about the article I had written for *Measure* and the sources on which it was based, because I had consulted him about it. He had spoken with Leonard Zakim at the Anti-Defamation League. Zakim telephoned me a few days later. "You are not alone," he said. "We will see that you are defended." He had made arrangements for me to have a pro bono defense by Robert Popeo, one of the top trial lawyers in Boston, a partner in the firm of Mintz, Levin, Ferris, Glovsky, and Popeo.

Zakim took me to meet Bob Popeo and his partner, Henry Sullivan, who would be in charge of the case. "You did the right thing," Popeo said, "and we will defend you. We will not settle." Ordinarily, I learned, people were eager to settle lawsuits for reasonable sums to avoid the high cost of litigation, which could have topped $100,000 in 1994. Many lawsuits were filed in the hope of getting a cash settlement. But Popeo said that if Martin had hoped to make five or ten thousand dollars in this way, he would be disappointed.

Here at last were people who could appreciate what I had been trying to do. Outside of academe, apparently, it was easier to understand the rights and wrongs of the controversy. Inside it, on the other hand, this distinction still seemed hopelessly muddled. The sympathy that these high-powered lawyers expressed was almost too much for me. At Wellesley I had managed to stay outwardly calm, even when Martin gave his speech denouncing me in the Academic Council, and even when various members of the administration had been impatient with me. But now that people were prepared to praise what I had done, rather than to shun me or anxiously change the subject, the tears I'd worked so hard to hold back came to my eyes.

The lawsuit, Henry Sullivan explained, was wholly without merit. It would be hard for Martin to show that he had been damaged by anything I had said, since he had not lost his job or a significant amount of income. Sullivan thought that Martin was simply trying to silence me, because once I was a defendant it would be unwise for me to say anything about him or about the case under litigation. The lawsuit would also discourage other people from trying to criticize him.

Sullivan also believed that the lawsuit was intended as a form of harassment. Normally a person who thought he had been libeled would sue the publication as well as the author, but Martin had chosen to sue only me, not *Measure,* the periodical in which the article had appeared. Strikingly, he had failed to sue or even to mention *Heterodoxy,* which had published the article that I cited as my source in my description of the confrontation between him and Plantec. Why only me and not the others? Why didn't Martin ask for a published apology, if he could show that the statement was substantially incorrect? And could he show that?

Nor could the possibility be ruled out that I had been sued because I was Jewish. Martin appeared to believe that Jews were responsible for the African slave trade. If so, it would follow that if their descendants had profited from their ancestors' crimes, they should be prepared to pay reparations to their descendants.

I told the lawyers how I came to write the article in question and what I had learned about the incident since. The editor of *Measure* had written to me in June 1993 asking me to comment on the events at Wellesley. *Measure* was an inexpensively produced newsletter, founded by Sidney Hook (1902–89), a philosopher who had started out as a Communist and then rejected

Marxism in favor of political conservatism. But since articles in recent issues of the newsletter seemed concerned primarily with academic responsibility, and some famous people were listed as subscribers, I agreed to write a short article, which I titled "Hurt Feelings at Wellesley."

The article summarized the events and controversies that I have described in the preceding chapters. I argued that the main reason why people were avoiding the issue of what was being taught to students was that "no one wanted to contradict or question any decision by Prof. Martin. Recently he has responded angrily to the most innocent of questions."[3] My first example was the incident in which Martin had reportedly shouted at Michelle Plantec in the residence hall, but I also described occasions when Martin had directed his anger against me.

I had heard about the Plantec incident in the winter of 1992–93 from Margery Sabin, a colleague in the English Department. In October 1991 she had been at the reading of Shakespeare's *Twelfth Night* in the residence hall where the incident occurred. She herself had not witnessed the confrontation, but she thought the college had not done enough to support Michelle Plantec. I'd also heard essentially the same story from Alyson Todd, a senior at Wellesley. I knew Todd well, because she had written to me in spring 1992 to express her dismay at what Martin and some of his students had been saying about me. She had even helped me briefly as a research assistant. In the fall of 1992, Todd told me she planned to write about the Plantec incident. She knew some of the witnesses and meant to talk to the head of house at the residence hall. It sounded to me as if she intended to do her homework.

In July 1993, when I wrote the disputed article in *Measure*, I had a new source to draw on, an article in *Heterodoxy*, a monthly newspaper that was outspokenly critical of the current vogue for political correctness in the academic world.[4] The article, "Blacks and Jews and All the News," had been written by Alyson Todd, who had just graduated. As her source she cited the article by Jennifer Paull and her colleagues in *Galenstone* that featured the interviews with both Martin and Michelle Plantec.[5] Because of a "code of silence" imposed by the administration of the college, Todd explained, it was not until May 1993 that the interviews with Martin and Plantec were published. Todd was particularly critical of President Keohane in her article. In her view, Keohane "has chosen to look the other way while still issuing platitudes about diversity."

I didn't see the *Galenstone* article when it came out, because few copies ever made it to Founders Hall, the building where my office was located. I tried to find one in the library, without success (it is not listed in the library catalogue). I even tried to scrounge one up in the department office, in case a copy had been sent there, but that part of Founders Hall had been closed for the summer because of construction. Then I tried to call Todd at her home in Maryland, again without success.

I also tried to reach Michelle Plantec. I found an address in an old college directory and wrote to her, but the letter was returned to me a few weeks later, addressee unknown.

At first, I quoted rather than summarized the relevant section of Todd's article, including the part about Plantec falling down during the confrontation with Martin, in an early draft of my essay for *Measure*. Later, I took the quotation marks out, and instead cited her article as the source of my information in an endnote. I did this because I was in England that summer while I was finishing my final draft, and I didn't have the text of her article with me with which to verify the quotation. Unfortunately, and despite my citation of the source I had used, it then became possible to allege that the words were mine rather than Alyson Todd's.

When I finally was able to track down Alyson Todd, she claimed that she had not written that Plantec fell down, but that the editors of *Heterodoxy* had rewritten her article. She had not said anything about her falling down in an early draft. Rather, she had simply summarized a statement by Mindy Nierenburg, the head of house in Claflin Hall. Nierenburg said that Martin had backed Plantec against a wall and, while pointing his finger in her face, uttered a stream of abuse, including such phrases as "bigot" and "fucking bitch." After trying unsuccessfully to stand between Martin and Plantec, Nierenburg had called the police. She later wrote to Gwenn Bookman, the college's affirmative action officer: "A Wellesley College Professor cannot be permitted to respond to a Wellesley student in this manner."

New software made it easier for faculty to access college records, so I was finally able to reach Michelle Plantec's mother, Adele, in Los Angeles. Michelle hadn't *fallen* down, she said; she had retreated *backward* down the stairs until her back was against a wall.

The family had promised not to reveal the details of the financial settlement the college had made with them when their daughter left, but she could send me other documents, including letters the college had solicited from eyewitnesses, and I would find that these letters supported her daughter's statement. A few days later I spoke with Michelle herself, who was now at the University of Southern California. She still found it painful to talk about the incident.

In the materials the college had sent to the Plantec family that Michelle's mother forwarded to me, student witnesses confirmed the head of house Mindy Nierenburg's account of the incident. One mentioned that Martin had "towered over" Plantec. He could hardly have done otherwise, since he is taller than most women. So it was effectively true that he had "bent over her" and that he was angry with her. The phrase "fucking white bitch" used by *Heterodoxy* was the semantic equivalent of "bigot" plus "fucking bitch."

In retrospect, it may have been significant that Plantec was Jewish. There is no reason to suppose that Martin could have known she was Jewish simply by looking at her. But her parents evidently thought that anti-Semitism might have been involved, because in 1991 they contacted the New York office of the American Jewish Committee, "complaining about Martin and his verbal harassment," and Martin Goldman of the Boston office had looked into the matter.[6] Michelle Plantec said that she had wanted Sally Greenberg, the legal counsel of the New England branch of the ADL, to represent her at the mediation meeting with Martin that never took place.[7] In view of what happened later, it is not unthinkable that Martin could have learned about Plantec's ethnicity sometime after his encounter with her in the residence hall.

CHAPTER SEVEN

Reparations?

etermining exactly what had happened in the residence hall in 1991 was just one aspect of what would be a long and demanding process. For five and a half years, until Martin's lawsuit against me was finally dismissed in 1999, I was on constant call to answer questions. My lawyers had to be able to reach me wherever my travels took me. Lawyers, of course, know how to deal with the pressure of constant interrogatories, briefs, and memoranda, just as academics learn not to panic when they receive a large stack of student papers. But all the legal procedures were new to me, and more than occasionally stressful.

During the first two years there was no real progress. We moved to have the case dismissed on summary judgment by the court, without having it come to trial. Judge Charles T. Spurlock of the Middlesex Superior Court, who as it happens is an African American, found in our favor, but Martin appealed.[1] The case then went to mediation, but Martin was not satisfied with the mediator's recommendation. The case was then sent back to the lower court, and moved into "discovery" phase.

We needed to obtain (and eventually received) Wellesley's records, in order to supplement the materials that Adele Plantec had sent us two years earlier. We needed to confirm that the plaintiff (Martin) was a "public figure." If he was (and most published authors could be regarded as at least "limited purpose" public figures), he would be required to show not just that what I wrote was untrue, but that I had insisted on publishing it anyway with "reckless disregard to whether it was false or true." We also needed to hear his side of the Plantec incident story, and to determine whether he had suffered damage to his livelihood specifically because of what I had said.

It was also necessary for both Martin and me to testify under oath at depositions, a process of the law known as "discovery." At his deposition in October 1996 Martin conceded that he was a public figure. Before the *Measure* article had appeared in the fall of 1993 he had appeared as a guest on several national television shows, and had been the subject of articles in major newspapers.

As for damages to his livelihood, Martin's tax returns for 1990–94 showed a substantial gain in income in 1993 and 1994. He said he had not consulted a doctor or a psychiatrist. All he could produce in support of his claim of damages was a letter from Rubin Patterson, a sociologist at the University of Toledo, who claimed that Martin had lost an opportunity to become director of Africana Studies at the University of Toledo because of charges of, as the letter stated, "what might be called 'academic licentiousness.' The initial pieces of literature that arrived on campus, as I recall, were from *Measure* and *Counterpoint*."[2]

In fact, however, the reason Martin did not get the job at Toledo in the summer of 1995 was because of his by then well known anti-Semitism. Martin was simultaneously being considered for a joint appointment in the History Department there, which was important for him because at Wellesley his courses were no longer cross-listed by the History Department. A professor of history at the University of Toledo, Robert Freeman-Smith, noticed that among Martin's publications was a book called *The Jewish Onslaught*.[3] Freeman-Smith remembered having read something in *Measure* about Martin's use of *The Secret Relationship*. Freeman-Smith then contacted a leader of the Jewish community, who in turn contacted the ADL. By then, the ADL had a whole file on Martin, including a pamphlet with a selection of his anti-Semitic statements, titled "Tony Martin in His Own Words." The administration of the University of Toledo then decided to terminate Martin's candidacy. The university was not willing to risk having a person known for anti-Semitism on its faculty.

As for the encounter with Plantec, Martin's story appeared to be at variance with what Plantec and other witnesses had said.[4] The others had heard her say, "Excuse me, sir, who are you with?" But Martin claimed that someone had been yelling at him in a loud, "hostile," "offensive," and "racist" manner. This woman moved toward him "aggressively," and continued to yell at him. He said that he turned and told her that she was a "racist little bigot," though then he thought that he might not have said "little" and "bigot." He didn't point at her, according to his account; she never stepped backward; his comments were brief.

This story was also at odds with the account of the incident given on November 6, 1991, to President Keohane by six faculty members (including Martin) and the undergraduate head of the black student association Ethos. These seven had written a letter to Keohane calling her attention to what they saw as a pattern of "widespread harassment of black males on this campus." Although none of the writers except Martin had witnessed the incident, they stated:

> On his way back to the reception he was rudely accosted by two women. They shouted at him in a hostile and aggressive manner. . . . Professor Martin's first reaction was to ignore the shouting women as he felt no obligation to respond to such uncivil behavior.[5]

If the second shouting student in fact existed, it is curious that she was never identified by any other witness.

Martin expressed no remorse about Plantec's departure from Wellesley in the deposition. He insisted that her remarks were racist, even though she had not used any specifically racial words.

Martin claimed that I had been hostile toward him from the time that my article appeared in the *New Republic.* He believed that my publication of the *Measure* article was an "escalation" of these hostilities. Here it was clear that he intended to argue as a legal matter that I had been negligent because I did not question the accuracy of the *Heterodoxy* article, or look up the transcript of the interviews in *Galenstone.*

In December 1996 it was my turn to be deposed. Martin and his lawyer had three goals for the deposition: to see what kind of witness I would make, to establish (if they could) that I was a racist, and, most importantly for their purposes, to show that I bore malice toward Martin and knew that what I had written in *Measure* was untrue. This, if they could prove it, would be the key to their claim of defamation.

Tony Martin chose to attend the deposition. He sat watching me disapprovingly from across the table. His attorney, Winston Kendall, wanted to know if I was "a member" of any Jewish advocacy groups, what Jewish groups I supported, and the amount of that support (modest). Why had I been given an award by the ADL in May 1996? (Because I took a stand against anti-Semitism.) Could I define anti-Semitism? Did I believe there was a conspiracy against Martin at Wellesley? (No.) Did I send students to audit his classes? (No.) Did I know David Horowitz, the publisher of *Heterodoxy,* who was also on the board of advisers of *Counterpoint*? (No, because the board never met.) Had I been consulted about the article written by *Counterpoint* editor Avik Roy about Martin's lawsuits against the college? (No.)

Kendall sought continually to bring the issue of race into the discussion. Could I describe the defendant? Was that, I wondered, so they could accuse me of racism if I said he was black? Kendall was determined to find evidence of prejudice. Before the afternoon session of the deposition resumed, he commented that he was surprised that he and Martin had even been allowed into the offices of Mintz, Levin, the law firm defending me, because they were two "big black men."

In response to further questions, I explained how I had

tried to find out more about the Plantec incident before I sent in the final copy of my *Measure* article. I told the lawyers why I had been unable to locate the *Galenstone* issue or Todd or Plantec, and of conversations I had had with Margery Sabin in the English Department, who had been present at the play reading, as well as with Gwenn Bookman, who told me that student records were confidential. I had not spoken to Mindy Nierenburg because I did not know until after I wrote the article that she had been involved.

In the official police report about the confrontation between Martin and Plantec, the reporting officer, Sergeant Carrie J. Valdes, had described the encounter as an "understanding [*sic*] about not knowing Mr. Martin was going downstairs w/ permission."[6] Kendall wanted to show that I had been negligent because I did not obtain a copy of the full police report of the incident before writing about it. But the reason I had never seen it is that it was a confidential document, not available to persons who were not involved in the event or to the public outside a legal context. Martin had a copy because he was one of the parties involved in the incident.

Although nothing that I said could have been very useful to Martin or his attorney, the deposition went on for a very long time, with intense questioning and numerous insinuations about deceit and racism. It was exhausting. I came away utterly drained from the aggressiveness of the interrogation and the hostility and anger that lay behind it.

A few days later, Kendall asked for documentation in support of virtually everything that I had said at the deposition. The list included requests for two copies of everything I had written between 1988 and 1995. I couldn't help wondering if Martin and Kendall really meant to slog through all my writings on classical subjects. What was the nature of the award given to me by the New England Chapter of ADL in April 1996? (A framed print.) Did I receive payments from the ADL? I wished there had been some way to ask him why he supposed the ADL would have paid me. Did the Nation of Islam pay professors who were helpful to them?

Martin had played the role of Duke Orsino in the reading of *Twelfth Night* at Claflin Hall in 1991. I couldn't help wondering if he shouldn't have been cast as the angry and vengeful Malvolio. While I should have been reading sixty-some student papers and turning in my grades for that semester, I was busy rummaging around for hours to find answers to questions in long and repetitive interrogatories.

In March 1997 we filed for a summary judgment, a request to the court that the case be dismissed for lack of substance before coming to trial. Finally, in January 1998, Judge Regina Quinlan of the Middlesex Superior Court allowed our motion.[7] She understood that I had used my description of the Plantec incident to illustrate a legitimate point: That the plaintiff was able to get away with using a controversial textbook free of any interference from other faculty because they did not wish to antagonize him for fear of an angry reaction. The discussion of the use of the book stemmed from the plaintiff's public status as a teacher of Afrocentrism, and the defendant was entitled to take issue with the use of the book and to explore why and how the plaintiff had managed to continue using it without having to answer for his choice.

Judge Quinlan concluded that the plaintiff was unlikely to be able to show that I had acted with reckless disregard or knowledge of falsehood. "Summary judgment is therefore appropriate," she wrote.

Once again Martin appealed. This time, though not until May 1999, the Massachusetts Court of Appeals upheld the judgment of the lower court. As a public figure, Martin needed to be able to show that I had acted with reckless disregard for whether what I said was true or false, and, in the words of the court's ruling, "he has shown no reasonable expectation of being able to sustain his burden at trial."[8] Martin did not seek further appellate review.

So the case was closed, without fanfare or any notice in the newspapers. In March 1998, in his "Broadside" no. 4, Martin had boasted that he had won the second round in his libel suit against me, and then noted as if in passing that I had won round three in a successful motion for summary judgment. In describing this last phase of the legal saga, he claimed: "Lefkowitz admitted that the offending words she wrote about Martin were untrue."[9] This was false: I had admitted no such thing.

Martin also lost his case against Avik Roy, another detail that he neglected to record in his "Broadside." That story was given full coverage in the *Chronicle of Higher Education,* which made the electronic text of the decision available on its Web site. Judge Judith Fabricant ruled that Roy's article was substantially true, that he had not written the article with malice, and that Martin had failed to show that either his reputation or his health had been damaged by the publication.[10]

Roy, as had I, pointed out that Martin's history of suing

people might have explained the college's hands-off approach toward him. Martin appealed the case, but in 2002 the Appeals Court upheld the lower court's decision.[11] Martin's case against Wellesley College for denying him a merit increase was dismissed on summary judgment.[12]

I could not help reflecting how much more fortunate I had been than Michelle Plantec. Jewish advocacy groups went out of their way to help me, and I had the generous legal assistance of one of the top law firms in Boston, as well as a principled and effective response from my insurance company. As Leonard Zakim of the ADL had said to me, causing me almost to break down and weep, I was not alone.

I still regret that such effective support had not been there for Plantec. She could easily have been defended as well, had some of us known about her case. On some college campuses, hostile words have been regarded as a form of virtual assault. "Words that wound," when used as weapons, can be treated with the kind of seriousness that would be appropriate in response to acts of physical violence.[13]

This legal strategy was devised for victims of racist speech acts, who were thought to be even more vulnerable to such abuse than members of the majority population.[14] Yet if anyone in the incident at the residence hall of Wellesley had uttered words that wound, it was Martin. If he had been at the University of Wisconsin at the time, he would have been sanctioned for shouting "fucking bitch" at a female student.[15] The "words that wound" strategy could reasonably have been employed in defense of Plantec, on the grounds that she was less powerful than Martin, and inferior both in status and in experience, and of course a female in a context where the presence of males was potentially dangerous.

At the very least, intervention on Plantec's behalf would have called attention to the defects in our advising system, and encouraged public debate of the incident. In fact, more public openness and debate all around would have encouraged all of us to think about how to deal with such an issue. It was precisely the hush-up, settle, and impose confidentiality approach that had almost prevented the issues in this case from being aired clearly and in public. My lawyers all felt that Martin's litigation was part of his strategy to maintain secrecy and perpetuate confusion.

Mainly what I learned from my brush with the law was that academics should not expect courts to come to their rescue, even though in my case they eventually did, after some years. It is far better for educators to address such questions themselves in honest debate. We need to compel ourselves to do so.

Discussion is a much more effective way to resolve academic disputes than litigation, which is slow and cumbersome, and extremely expensive, demanding time, energy, and money that most people do not have. Litigation silences criticism, and discourages future criticism. In the end, the worst aspect of *Martin v. Lefkowitz* was not the fact that it was painful for me and my family to live through. It was that it prevented a learning process that would have been of benefit to both faculty and students. From that point of view, the silence surrounding the Plantec incident was even worse.

CHAPTER EIGHT

A Racist Polemic?

At the same time that I began to learn more about the incident involving Michelle Plantec and Tony Martin, in the summer of 1993, I discovered the source of the myth of the Stolen Legacy. It was a historical novel, a fictional narrative written by a classical scholar who made explicit and specific use of ancient sources. Unfortunately the historical information it presented was almost entirely without value, because it was published in 1731, nearly a century before the decipherment of hieroglyphics made it possible to read sources written in ancient Egyptian and to see what the Egyptians themselves were saying. In other words, the source of the Stolen Legacy myth was not ancient, not historical, and not African. It was historical fiction.

Sethos: A History or Biography, Based on Unpublished Memoirs of Ancient Egypt, by the Abbé Jean Terrasson, is now justifiably forgotten, but in its day it was something of a best seller.[1] It derived much of its appeal from its imaginative description of religious education in ancient Egypt. Ancient Memphis, as Terrasson imagined it, was a university town, with buildings connected by underground passages, galleries, museums, laboratories, gardens, a large outdoor zoo, and schools of astronomy and geometry, that anticipated and surpassed the schools in Athens of Plato, Aristotle, and their pupils.

A central feature of the novel is its description of the Egyptian Mysteries, with elaborate initiation rituals and lofty educational goals.[2] Approaching religion through reason and education held a particular appeal to intellectuals in eighteenth-century Europe, among them some prominent Freemasons. The Masons were eager to recreate in their own rituals some of the features of Terrasson's Egyptian Mystery System.

People lost interest in *Sethos* once it became possible to know more about the actual life in ancient Egypt. The most significant addition to modern knowledge about Egypt came in 1824, when Jean-François Champollion (1790–1832) published the first dictionary of hieroglyphics. As time went on and more new texts could be read, it became increasingly clear that Greek travelers, starting with Herodotus in the fifth century, had only a partial understanding of what they had seen.

After Egyptian hieroglyphics could be read it became clear that, whatever the fanciful speculations of earlier scholars, historians, and novelists, there had never been an Egyptian Mystery System (EMS), nor any educational infrastructure to support it. The popularity of speculations like Terrasson's and the Free-masons' then ceased. There is no evidence that the eclipse of the EMS idea was the result of racism or any prejudiced repudia-tion of African influence on European culture. Champollion, the scholar whose study of hieroglyphics effectively made all subse-quent discoveries possible, was interested not in colonization or triumphalism, but simply in learning as much as he could about what had happened in the past.[3] After he had shown that his sys-tem of deciphering hieroglyphics worked, he traveled to Egypt to see the monuments for himself. Because he spoke Arabic fluently he lived and worked with the local population.

I discuss the connection between Terrasson and the myth of the Stolen Legacy in close detail in my book *Not Out of Af-rica,* published in 1996.[4] The title (borrowed from my 1992 *New Republic* review) was memorable, but easy to misconstrue. It has been thought to mean that "no good thing comes from Africa," or that I think *homo sapiens* originated in some place other than Africa, even though the book does not discuss that subject.

The book's title did not get me in nearly so much trouble as its cover. Originally the publisher had planned to use a cover showing the statue of Aphrodite of Melos (the so-called Vénus de Milo) against a background of Kente cloth. But at the last minute, Basic Books substituted the old *New Republic* cover, showing a bust of a Greek philosopher wearing a Malcolm X cap, with highlights in purple. People who were prepared to judge books by their covers assumed that *Not Out of Africa* was meant to shock.

Fortunately many people managed to get past the cover and look at what I actually had to say. I first explained why it was unlikely and even impossible that the immediate ancestors of figures like Socrates and Cleopatra could have been black. I explained at length why stories of Greek philosophers visiting Egypt were almost certainly not true, and pointed out that even if they had gone there, they would not have learned about Greek philosophy. If I were writing the book again, I would have quoted more extensively from the writings of Egyptian and Greek thinkers. Egyptian texts describing the gods are profound and complex, but they do not employ the abstract, non-theological terminology characteristic of the writings of Plato and Aristotle.

In the second half of the book I talked about the development of the notion that there had once been Egyptian Mysteries similar to the initiation cults characteristic of Greece and Rome, and discussed Terrasson's novel *Sethos* and its influence on Freemasonry. Then I reviewed all the statements about the Egyptian origins of Greek philosophy made by George G. M. James in *Stolen Legacy,* showing how his entire thesis was based on the mythology of Freemasonry, and that many of the works cited in support of his arguments did not in fact offer any support for his claims.

If the book had dealt with an issue of interest only to classical scholars, it would not have caused a stir. But because most Afrocentrists are black and the myth of the Stolen Legacy has been a source of pride and empowerment, race quickly became the dominant factor in the discussion of the issues raised by the book, even though the book made no judgments about individuals or races but only about ideas. It hadn't been the greatest pleasure to be a defendant in a lawsuit, or to be the target of anti-Semitic slurs. But all that would prove to be low-key in comparison with the controversy aroused by the publication of *Not Out of Africa.*

The techniques of argument used by my critics have been employed and will continue to be used by anyone with any kind of ethnocentric theory. They are easy to use, because they require no deep knowledge of the subject under discussion. And they work, at least with some audiences, and are particularly effective in the short run.

The approach runs something like this: (1) So far as possible, stay away from the facts, since few if any supporting data can be found to confirm fundamentally racial theories. (2) Keep your readers' attention on racism, because you can seize a moral high ground by using the powerful trump card of race. You can even claim that your opponents are themselves racist or unwittingly inspired by racist motives. (3) Never underestimate the power of myth, which is easier to grasp than history and appeals directly to the emotions.[5]

Inevitably the most effective response to *Not Out of Africa* was to play the race card. One of the most determined efforts came from Selwyn Cudjoe, the colleague in Wellesley's Africana Studies Department with whom I had worked in 1992 to hold discussions about *Black Athena* and to bring Martin Bernal to Wellesley. Cudjoe had spoken out strongly against anti-Semitism. But he now spoke out equally vigorously against my book, although without ever coming to grips with its main arguments.

A few months after *Not Out of Africa* was published, Cudjoe wrote an op-ed essay for the *Boston Globe* in which he claimed that in *Not Out of Africa* I was trying "to debunk everything that black scholars have accomplished over the past 30 years." (*Every-thing* accomplished in the whole field of African-American stud-ies, that is, in a book that focused exclusively on ancient history.) He went on to imply that I had launched a personal attack against him and his fellow Afrocentrists *because they were black.*

> She and her colleagues (mostly white) are correct because they have the "facts" at their disposal. My colleagues and I (mostly black) are extreme Afro-centrists whose capacity for rational thought is se-verely restricted.[6]

Of course I had said no such thing in *Not Out of Africa* or in the article I wrote for the *Chronicle of Higher Education* in 1993 about the Stolen Legacy theory, or anywhere else.[7] By putting scare quotes around the word "facts," Cudjoe suggested that they were not important. Pejorative labeling is always a useful strategy if the facts do not support your argument.[8]

In May 1996, a few months after *Not Out of Africa* was published, Cudjoe organized a teach-in at Wellesley with the title "Just Out of Africa."[9] He invited me to speak, and at my request he also included my ancient historian colleague Guy Rogers. But the other six speakers represented opposing points of view.

According to Alice Dembner, then education editor of the *Boston Globe,* who attended the teach-in, Cudjoe said he had organized the event because his students felt "their discipline was being trashed." He characterized the two-hour session as "a battle between two camps for social and historical meaning, *not merely an excavation of facts*" (italics added). Again he kept the focus on the perceived threat of my work to Africana Studies *as a whole.*

He appealed to the emotions of his audience (many of whom had been bused in from other campuses) by using the rhetoric of destruction ("trashed") and war ("battle between two camps").

In his op-ed for the *Boston Globe* Cudjoe preferred to talk about possibilities. Even though there was no way to document how ideas could have come from Egypt to Greece, it still might have been *possible* for such borrowing to have occurred. He complained that I seemed to be saying that "all knowledge can be reduced to texts, that libraries are always coterminous with buildings and that the cross-fertilization of ideas stopped at the Egyptian borders."

Without a doubt one can do much more with possibilities than with evidence. Possibilities can be molded, shaped, or adapted as the occasion requires.[10] That is why Bernal in all his discussions about the past kept referring to the need for scholars of antiquity to speak of competitive plausibilities rather than history. It is this flexibility that endows postmodern criticism with its protean power. Postmodernist discourse allows anyone with rhetorical skills to be able to hold forth persuasively on any topic, provided that he or she keeps the discussion at a certain level of generality. Although it makes little or no sense to talk about Africa or Europe as if they were unified entities in the fifth century B.C., in his *Boston Globe* piece Cudjoe, a specialist in the literature of the Caribbean, confidently asserted:

> Lefkowitz blames Afrocentrists for taking Herodotus more seriously than he took himself even though he lived and traveled throughout Africa in the period of which Lefkowitz speaks.[11]

Herodotus himself gives a different account of his travels. The known world in his day consisted of the Mediterranean Sea and the peoples who lived in some proximity to it. He was completely unaware of the full geography of the vast continent of Africa. He says that he traveled up the Nile, but no farther than its first cataract, at Elephantine (modern-day Aswan), near what was at the time the border between Egypt and Nubia, some 550 miles south of modern Cairo. It was rather like saying that, by traveling from Washington to Boston, one had toured the whole continent of North America.

Why is it that Cudjoe assumed that Herodotus knew about the rest of Africa? Or that he was likely to know better than a classicist or an Egyptologist what the Greek text says? Perhaps he supposed that knowledge of Africa was something you were *born* into, by virtue of being of African descent? As another speaker, Constance Hilliard, said at the teach-in, "truth isn't something you find in a library . . . you have to open your soul."[12] When scholars of African descent talked about the inability of scholars of European descent to judge African civilization with anything like objectivity, they weren't just speaking figuratively. They meant it literally.

Although it is fundamentally racist to judge people by their ancestry rather than by their knowledge or other skills, in these discussions race was frequently invoked as a valid qualification for the interpretation of historical and historiographical issues.[13] During these strange days in the academy it seemed that race had become knowledge. Descartes had said, "I think; therefore I exist" (*cogito, ergo sum*). Now the motto had become: "I am, therefore I know" (*sum, ergo scio*). This transformation had occurred not just in the field of African-American studies, but in many other areas of ethnic inquiry as well. Yet isn't it absurd to suppose that only a Jew could understand what it means and has meant for all time to be Jewish? It might help to have been a Jew or to know Jews well, but any deep knowledge of Jewish studies still requires learning and reflection, which can be obtained by anyone of any background who is willing and able to do the necessary work.

In the study of ancient history, especially, being cannot be a way of knowing. The only way one can learn about the ancient world is by studying its surviving texts and artifacts. We have no other choice. We have not lived in antiquity or in the settings of civilizations like those found in the ancient world. Identity politics are not an option. This approach belongs where it came from, in the modern world.

But Afrocentrists, by treating ancient Egypt as synonymous (somehow) with modern Africa, inserted it into the politics of the present. Evidently they felt they had acquired the authority to talk about it, because identity is a job qualification in many departments of Africana studies. That meant because I was white (or maybe because I was Jewish) I automatically lacked the necessary credentials to talk about an African past.

In October 1996, before a lecture I gave at the University of California at Davis, I happened to overhear a young black man telling a friend to come to my talk because "she has to be *corrected.*" At the lecture, black students and faculty distributed xeroxed sheets with pictures of ancient black people. Afterward people in the audience told me that they thought these sheets were the handout I had prepared to illustrate my talk. But my talk had nothing to do with the race of the ancient Egyptians. My topic was the myth of the Stolen Legacy.

Still, in distributing their papers, and asking questions after the lecture, the students at UC Davis had chosen to exercise their freedom of speech in an orderly and appropriate manner. In April 1997 at San Diego State University, the tactics were not so polite. There a full-fledged protest was organized against me, including students who were walking up and down before the lecture hall carrying placards.

Nonetheless, the people inside the auditorium listened to my lecture and asked some good questions. Khallid Muhammad was there in person, and I shook hands with him. But the tone changed a couple of hours later, after I had left and he was the speaker to the African Student Union at the university. The talk was billed as "Dr. Khallid Muhammad. Black Man. 'Not Out of Europe.' Too Black, Too Strong."

In his talk he brought up all the anti-Semitic and racist themes characteristic of his speeches at various universities. Again he indulged in wordplay: "Dikeda Left-o-witch."[14] Then came the insults. I was "a homosexual . . . imposter man . . . imposter Jew," a "hook-nosed, lox-eating, bagel-eating . . . something . . . something . . . so called Jew." Again there was that old idea about fake European Jews that had surfaced in ben-Jochannan's presentation at Wellesley. Also, like Leonard Jeffries, Muhammad clearly did not approve of homosexuals.[15] (I don't particularly like bagels, and I am not a homosexual, though I rather liked being thought of as one.) But I supposed it all just went to show how patently absurd ideas can flourish in an atmosphere where people accept, or become entranced by, the idea that facts don't matter.

To their credit, the students of the SDSU Secular Society and the Afro-American Studies Department didn't just go away muttering about how hopeless it all was, as my colleagues had done when ben-Jochannan made his remarks about hook-nosed Jews at Wellesley. So in the end perhaps more good than harm was done by my lecture and the subsequent discussion of Muhammad's "commentary" on it. The Secular Society students distributed their own fliers denouncing Muhammad's talk, stressing the need for open dialogue rather than "race-bashing revival meetings."

The SDSU Secular Society understood why black student organizations wanted to invite figures like Khallid Muhammad to their campuses. Nothing unites people like a common enemy. Speakers like Muhammad, Leonard Jeffries, and Tony Martin in their different ways were skilled in encouraging black unity, both by summoning up visions of Africa's glorious past and by providing justifications for hating Jews in particular and whites in general.

Sometimes these black unity meetings took the slightly less confrontational form of a football rally. In March 1996 the New York radio station WBAI invited Guy Rogers and me to debate Martin Bernal and John Henrik Clarke. When we got there, we discovered that the audience had been bused in especially for the debate. Eutrice Leid, who was supposed to act as the moderator, was clearly in favor of the side represented by Bernal and Clarke. As Rogers memorably put it, "This is an away game."

The writer Robert Boynton was in the audience, and he later reported that Clarke began by stating (to wild applause): "I am not here to debate, because I only debate with my equals."[16]

Not Out of Africa was "a good sophomore effort," but basically "nothing more than a rationalization for the re-enslavement of the African people." Apparently, according to Clarke, my saying that Aristotle didn't steal his philosophy from Egypt meant that I wanted to re-enslave Africans. It seemed as if a criticism of the work of one black writer by a white person could be construed as a comprehensive attack on *all* black people.

As moderator, Leid did not so much ask questions as level a series of accusations at us. She had it in for me, especially, because I had never been to Africa. Anything Rogers or I said was greeted by boos and catcalls. Toward the end Clarke threw in a few comments about the malevolence of Jews. I did not hear Bernal object to these remarks, even though in *Black Athena* he had been eager to find evidence of anti-Semitism in European classical scholarship.

Another charge against me was that *Not Out of Africa* had been praised by the conservative columnist George Will.[17] To Leid's audience, any association with the right wing of politics was the kiss of death. It is also anathema to most academics. Because many right-leaning writers praised the book, some academics concluded that my motivation for writing it must have been primarily political.[18]

However irrelevant framing the debate as a matter of politics was in reality, it furnished a convenient way to avoid discussing the historical problems raised by *Black Athena* and the idea of a Stolen Legacy. Instead of taking on the "formidable" task of reviewing the historical issues discussed in *Not Out of Africa* and *Black Athena Revisited,* Christopher Stray, who studies the sociology of classical studies, sought rather to "locate" them in

the contexts of the wider cultural debate to which they contributed.[19] Classicist David Konstan also believed that "which side
[Bernal and Lefkowitz] come down on reflects their personal
stances with respect to the politics of culture in our time."[20] If
only it had been that straightforward. The reality was that I had
no quarrel with Bernal's goal of lessening European "cultural
arrogance." I just didn't believe that misrepresenting what had
happened in the past was the right way or even the best way to
accomplish the task.

The debate wasn't, and never had been, about "politics." It
was about historical fact, and scholarship. By treating the matter
as if it were a political argument, critics were able to avoid discussing the historical issues, and the many inconvenient facts that
made the thesis of the Stolen Legacy impossible to maintain.

By treating *Not Out of Africa* as a political diatribe, the historian Wilson Jeremiah Moses was able to call my book "ahistori-
cal, presentist, synchronic, and absolutely devoid of the methods
of serious cultural or intellectual history." Just the possibility that
Not Out of Africa was somehow meant to disparage black people
or (worse) to hinder their social progress was enough for him to
justify classifying the book as the other side "of the same hateful
coin" represented by the writings of "black nationalist polemicist
Maulana Karenga."[21] Karenga, now best known as the creator of
the holiday Kwanzaa, had been a black-power advocate early in
his career.

Moses claims that, by debating me on National Public Radio and elsewhere, Karenga had assisted me, "once an obscure
drudge in the academic backwaters of a classics department, in
her quest for status as a 'public intellectual.'" Moses needed to

characterize me as an extremist so that he could distance himself both from me and from black extremists, and position himself as a moderate, using the classic tactic of triangulation. From this semblance of a middle point he characterizes Afrocentrism as a folk movement, with its own distinct cultural narrative. Although he recognizes that the thesis put forward in *Stolen Legacy* is pseudo-historical, he does not believe that it is harmful or advocates racial hatred, even though it is "filled with bitterness." Rather, it is an "admittedly idiosyncratic rhapsody," "an exotic but poignant attempt to unite African peoples with the rest of humanity, a moving response to segregation and dehumanization, the product of a heart filled with tears."[22]

Moses is surely justified in reminding his readers of the terrible conditions of Jim Crow education under which George G. M. James, the author of *Stolen Legacy,* was compelled to live and work. But that suffering does not redeem the damage that has been done by those who have encouraged their students to believe that *Stolen Legacy* was factual and historical. If you believe your legacy is stolen, what can you do but resent those who stole it, or be angry with those who insist that it wasn't really stolen after all? With his characterization of Afrocentrism as "a quaint folksy cultural tradition," Moses, as Clarence Walker has observed, tells only the happier side of the story.[23] Even though the Afrocentric myth of a Stolen Legacy may have been intended to bolster black pride, rather than to encourage hatred of whites, it can and has been used in that way by some of its proponents.

With this rhetoric Moses could count on eliciting the support of all academics who believed in the independent value of cultural narratives. This appeal to the sympathies of his readers may explain why his editors did not ask him to tone down his demeaning statements about me and about the discipline of classical studies. If I was tarred as an extremist, shows of even-handedness or good will toward me might have looked like an endorsement of racism.

Ironically, in their quest to find racism in everything they disapprove of, race professionals like Cudjoe, Martin, and Wilson too easily turn themselves into professional racists.[24] Often the charges the race pros make against their opponents could be more fairly used to characterize themselves. They are the demagogues, the seekers for public intellectual status, the ones who are concerned with the present rather than with the past.

The race professionals' appeals to theoretical considerations, such as definitions of methodology, are usually smoke-screens. They are still aware of the value of facts. They will mention supportive data, whenever they can, or attach references that impart an impression of authority. Wilson Moses observes that neither Bernal nor I refers to a rare 1853 Masonic pamphlet by Martin Delany. I duly tracked down and read Delany's work, but it turned out to have little relevance to the issues that we were discussing.[25]

Undoubtedly I did learn one significant lesson from all the criticism of my efforts in defense of the use of evidence in the writing of history. I saw how humiliating and miserable it is to be a victim of racism, to be hated for being a member of an outsider group (whether Jews or blacks), regardless of one's individual character or true intentions. I now know how frustrating it is to have motives attributed to me that never actually entered my mind, and to be treated unfairly and uncivilly.[26] In some debates, we but not our opponents were held to time limits. Audiences were stacked in our disfavor. I soon began to feel more like a football than a member of the visitors' team.

Being a victim of racism is indeed painful. How can you defend yourself if your fault is being Jewish, or of European descent? Still, I could go home at the end of the day and eventually get to sleep, because the racism I experienced took the form primarily of words and hot air. No one took my job away, or told me where I could or could not live. Even when I was sued and forced to defend myself, I was only a minor and temporary victim of verbal persecution. But that was enough to allow me to feel as well as understand both intellectually and emotionally what racism can do to the human mind and spirit.

CHAPTER NINE

Turning History into Fiction

B y now you may well be ready to say: Why put yourself through all this? The people you are defending have been dead for millennia. Most of the people you are trying to talk to won't listen to you. Or as an anonymous missive put it: "You. You so ugly. Why don't you sit down and shut up?"

Here's why. We owe it to the people of the past to record their history as accurately as we can. We owe it to ourselves to get as close to the truth as we can, whatever that truth turns out to be. If we allow ourselves or anyone to manipulate history, and rewrite it as they see fit, injustice will always be done to some people, either in the past or in the present. Historians would still believe that hieroglyphs were mystic symbols and that ancient

Egypt was par excellence the land of mystery, if Champollion had not worked long and hard to decipher that system of writing so that we could actually discover all that we do now know about ancient Egyptian religion and literature.

It is through the use of evidence that we can separate good scholarship from bad, in any field. The best argument is not the one we like, or the one that is argued most persuasively, but the one that offers the best account of all the available facts. What works in law courts works also in the writing of history, and indeed, law shares with history many tools in logic and honorable debate. You can't claim that a legacy is stolen if you cannot show that the claimant ever had the legacy to begin with.

In the case of ancient history the task is complicated. The evidence is often incomplete. The cultures are remote and difficult to understand. The ancient languages require years to learn properly. We can never know what happened then with the kind of precision we can now bring to bear on current events. But getting it ninety percent right is surely better than (say) ten percent or even none.

That is why I felt I had to say that the Stolen Legacy was myth rather than history, or that Jews were not the principal players in the slave trade. That is why I believed that it was imperative to come up with a comprehensive response to Bernal's *Black Athena*.[1] It is not that I had any objection to Bernal's professed goal of lessening European arrogance. Like almost every classicist I know, I was all in favor of making the study of the ancient world more comprehensive and inclusive. But I was persuaded that *Black Athena* offered a partial and biased account of the available evidence and had seriously misrepresented the intentions of classical scholars and ancient historians, both past and present.

Someone had to point out that classicists had discarded the idea that Egypt was the source of Greek wisdom, because it was not supported in the Egyptian source material. Bernal had presented numerous etymologies to support his hypothesis that many Greek words had derived from Egyptian, but to do so he appeared to have invented new linguistic rules that essentially allowed anything to be derived from anything. Although Bernal was persuaded that Egypt invaded Greece in the second millennium, he did not provide the material evidence to support this hypothesis. He had also presented distorted accounts of what European scholars thought, and throughout put his own ideas and words into their mouths. In some instances it looked as if he had not studied their work very closely.

Unfortunately in the climate of the 1990s it was not at all easy to explain why any of this mattered. Bernal's professed goals were so apparently noble, and his rhetoric so persuasive. By ingenious arguments and clever word choice he could turn history writing into a racial theory, or suggest that it was for "ideological" reasons that linguists refused to see that a large segment of ancient Greek vocabulary derived from ancient Egyptian.[2] He drove the point home by referring to what everyone else now calls the Indo-European language system as the "Aryan hypothesis," thus indirectly suggesting an affinity between Indo-European linguistics and Nazi theories of racial superiority, even though modern linguists take great care to disassociate language from "race." It did not really matter that he could marshal relatively little evidence to support his theories. The nature of his mission guaranteed that in any discussion Bernal would have the advantage of being able to resort, in the words of Paul R. Gross and Norman Levitt, "constantly and shamelessly to moral one-upmanship."[3] Anyone who tried to defend the traditional outlines of ancient history would ipso facto be acting in the interests of dead white European males, the forces of reaction, and so on.

Reading *Black Athena* was like stepping into a time machine. Suddenly it seemed as if one were back in the eighteenth or early nineteenth century, before people understood that Greek, Latin, and Sanskrit were part of the same language system, and that the origin or etymologies of words depended not on a general similarity of sound but on changes that could be plotted with some precision. Suddenly it was once again acceptable to treat myths as if they preserved an accurate memory of historical events, even though place names are in fact the only historical data that myths preserve with anything like fidelity.

Even Bernal's style of writing—egocentric, argumentative, rhetorical, insistent—seemed almost lively in comparison with the impersonal and flat style of so many professional articles on ancient subjects. *Black Athena* let its readers enter a less professional milieu where it was suddenly appropriate to promote one's own cause by directly attacking one's opponents' motives and credentials, and where amateur status was made to seem more respectable and honest than the work of hackneyed scholars.

These were some of the reasons why *Black Athena* was initially so successful. But Bernal also aided his cause by identifying himself with the academic left. At the same time, similar challenges were being mounted against the prevailing orthodoxies in virtually every academic subject, whether literary or in the natural and social sciences.[4] Even though they had long since ceased to occupy an important place in the university curriculum, the classics were particularly vulnerable because they were thought to be the foundational texts of Western Civilization, with all its perceived liabilities. Bernal did not seem to realize that the idea of a classics establishment was entirely fictional.[5] The subject now accommodates many different approaches and points of view.

Perhaps his most inspired offensive strategy was to make a virtue out of his lack of credentials in ancient history. He insisted that his work had caused a scientific revolution or "paradigm shift" in ancient studies. In scientific revolutions, he argued, it was often outsiders who brought about dramatic changes in thought.[6] Bernal did not point out that, to meet the criterion of a paradigm shift, a scientific theory must be rigorously tested and shown *to work.*[7]

Bernal also knew that he would have a better chance of winning if he could get everyone else to play by his rules. That meant dealing with competitive plausibilities rather than facts. Presumably he would pick the winning plausibility on the basis of its social utility. Why should the work of Afrocentrist cultural historians be considered any less valid than the work of "scientific" or "rationalistic" historians like myself, who are also, whether they realize it or not, fabricating narratives that may or may not correspond to what actually happened, which cannot be exactly known?[8]

It is just a short step from creating plausibility to writing historical fiction, and it is perhaps as a kind of historical novel that *Black Athena* should be remembered. It has many features in common with Terrasson's *Sethos*. Considerable learning went into the composition of both narratives, and both have a serious agenda to get across that pertains to their own times. Both narratives have episodes of preaching, and are not infrequently boring. Bernal's narrative is less coherent than Terrasson's, and his hero (himself) does not undergo a series of initiations and journeys in order to become a celibate priest. At times Bernal is a Virgil showing the reader around an Inferno populated by the racist souls of classical philologists and nineteenth-century novelists. At other times he is like Tamino in *The Magic Flute,* an opera inspired by *Sethos,* slaying dragons and fighting off demons as he rescues his bride, *Black Athena* herself.

Like Terrasson, Bernal was able to write a work of fiction that spoke to the unvoiced needs of some of his contemporaries. In the late 1980s and early 1990s many humanists and social scientists had begun to question the value of Western scientific achievements, on the grounds that they were a product of a racist and sexist culture. It was as if the moral authority of feminist and other minority viewpoints was enough to justify "bypassing the grubby necessities of actual scientific knowledge," as Gross and Levitt put it.[9]

Yet it seemed only too clear that Bernal had undertaken his enterprise on the basis of a false assumption. He had failed to see, or was prepared to overlook, the reason why classical scholars had abandoned the idea that ancient Egypt had an important influence on ancient Greek thought: There was no evidence for such a connection in the Egyptian source material that was made available after the decipherment of hieroglyphics. Terrasson's novel had been the source of the notion that there had once been Egyptian schools of philosophy, but it had been written a century before Champollion's work became widely accepted. While Bernal mentions Terrasson, he failed to see, or chose to disregard, the pivotal significance of Terrasson's historical fiction in the formation of the myth of the Stolen Legacy.[10] In the first volume of *Black Athena*, Bernal even appeared to believe in the existence of an actual Egyptian Mystery System in Middle or even Late Kingdom Egypt, and was ready to argue that Masonic rituals and other initiations derived from it.[11]

It was by no means easy to respond to such an out-of-date and tendentious attempt to rewrite ancient history. In every different subject area that Bernal discussed, someone with a professional background needed to review all the scientific reasons why mainstream scholars had long since discarded his hypotheses. It would take considerable patience and forbearing to prepare such thorough explanations. It was also clear that no single professional student of the ancient world had complete command of all the topics covered in *Black Athena*. A virtual team was needed to provide a comprehensive and thorough response. My ancient history colleague Guy Rogers joined me as co-editor of the volume *Black Athena Revisited*.[12] Together we set out to find scholars who shared our (and Bernal's) vision that the study of the ancient world should be truly multicultural and appreciative of the accomplishments of all ancient civilizations.

The volume we assembled left little doubt that the available evidence did not support Bernal's central claims. Egyptologists, although grateful to Bernal for drawing attention to their subject, showed that he did not possess an in-depth knowledge of Egyptian civilization or language.[13] They also pointed out that the written and archaeological evidence gave no support to his theory that Egypt had invaded Greece in the second millennium B.C.

Bernal's treatment of race also did not stand up to close

scrutiny.[14] Simply by nature of its geography Egypt was more closely linked to Western Asian cultures than it was to the rest of Africa. Egyptian was not cognate with other African languages, and in art the Egyptians distinguished themselves from other African and Asian peoples. Physical anthropology suggests that Egyptian physiognomies were somewhere between the types found to the north and south and east and west. If anything was clear, it was that the terms black, Egyptian, and Nubian ought not to be used as if they were interchangeable.

Because so much of Bernal's theory of Egyptian origin depended upon his ingenious etymologies, a review of Indo-European linguistics played a central role in *Black Athena Revisited*. In their essay "Word Games," the linguists Jay Jasanoff and Alan Nussbaum explained why scholars thought there had been a language or closely related languages called Proto-Indo-European. They provided illustrations of how scholars sought to discover the origin or etymology of particular words. Bernal's etymologies, by comparison, were not suggested by a study of comparative vocabularies and roots, but rather invented ad hoc to support his theory of Egyptian origin.[15] Jasanoff and Nussbaum concluded "that Bernal's claim to have uncovered 'hundreds' of viable Greek-Egyptian and Greek-Semitic etymologies is simply false."[16]

Another important essay discussed the question of Egyptian influence on Greek mathematics and science.[17] The issue was more complicated than Bernal had imagined. Mathematical astronomy was a Babylonian invention, further developed by Greeks with their rigorous demonstration procedures. Greek doctors used Egyptian drugs, but with different diagnostic methodologies.

Archaeological evidence provides further testimony to the intricate nature of cultural influence in the second millennium, in a world that (as a famous scholar of the Greek Bronze Age put it) had "no national borders, no passports, no strange currencies, no obstacle to travel and the acquisition of new cultural and artistic experiences."[18] The interrelation of ancient cultures was more complex than Bernal had supposed. Most Egyptian influence reached Greece indirectly, through the mediation of civilizations in the Near East, particularly in the Northern Levant, which traded with the Minoans in Crete and as well as with the Myceneans on the Greek mainland.

In evaluating individual artifacts and sites, one had to remember that familiarity with and admiration of another culture was a sign of appreciation rather than invasion. Again, it was clear that in insisting on one-way channels of communication Bernal had set out to prove a point, not to evaluate evidence objectively. He had tried to extract historical data from mythology, a practice that most modern scholars sedulously avoid, and took too little account of the important evidence provided by material artifacts like potsherds.

Other scholars evaluated Bernal's assessment of classical scholarship over the centuries. He did not appear to be fully aware that the Greeks themselves had different views of their own origins and derived multiple meanings from their own myths. He spoke about Greece, when in reality there were many distinct cultures within the ancient Greek world.[19] Similarly, Bernal had failed to recognize the great variety of attitudes expressed by eighteenth-century writers, and had not given sufficient recognition to national distinctions. Racism certainly existed in European

cultures after 1700, but always in conjunction with anti-racist
and abolitionist ideas and practices.[20] Although Bernal sought
to characterize eighteenth- and nineteenth-century classicists
as conservatives, a quiet revolution was taking place in ancient
studies during those centuries, as scholars sought to move the
study of history away from theology. In general Bernal relied too
heavily on individual portraits to characterize ages and nations,
and did not take sufficient account of information that did not
support his central thesis.[21]

In *Black Athena* Bernal was eager to find racism in German scholarship, and he appeared to have done so, at least in
several test cases. But in many of these instances that was only
one side of the story. In his discussion of this issue, for example,
Bernal said nothing about the anti-racist writings of the German
intellectual J. G. von Herder (1744–1803). The same might also
be said for his characterization of the English historian George
Grote (1794–1871).[22] Most strikingly, for all his determination to
discredit the "cultural arrogance" of European scholars, Bernal
appeared not to have noticed that the goal of giving credit to
Egypt for the "glory that was Greece" is in itself Eurocentric.[23]

Unfortunately, when we were collecting the essays in *Black
Athena Revisited,* Rogers and I did not know about and did not
include an important article by the Dutch ancient historian Josine
Blok. Blok had conducted a careful investigation of Bernal's assessment of the work of the German classical scholar Karl Otfried
Müller (1797–1840).[24] Müller was one of the first classical scholars
to argue that the Egyptian influence on ancient Greek culture was
more limited than the ancients had supposed. In *Black Athena*
Bernal suggested that Müller had been motivated by racism and

anti-Semitism. Blok showed that in fact Müller had great enthusiasm for ancient Egyptian and Hebrew cultures. Bernal had been
hampered in his discussion of Müller's writings because only a
small sample of them had been translated into English.

Virtually no aspect of Bernal's characterization of nineteenth-century European scholarship stood up to close scrutiny.
Yet this was the aspect of his work that was praised by many
academics, even by students of antiquity who were not persuaded
by his theories about Egypt and Greece. One can only suppose
that these scholars wanted Bernal's account of the nineteenth
century to be true. If he was correct, they could increase their
credibility by distancing themselves from the reprehensible attitudes of their predecessors, and they could join Bernal on the
moral high ground that he was so determined to claim. Trashing
nineteenth-century scholarship was a way of doing *something* (or
at least appearing to do something) about the shortcomings of
Western Civilization.

In such an intellectual climate, even completely absurd
propositions could seem persuasive, as long as they were clothed
in the right rhetoric and dropped the right academic names. In
1996 the physicist Alan Sokal demonstrated just how bad it could
get. Sokal sent an article to *Social Text,* a journal with editors sympathetic to the postmodernist interrogation of Western science.[25]
Sokal's article purported to show that gravity and other laws of
natural science were socially determined, that is, did not exist apart
from the fact that people *thought* they existed. Immediately after
the paper appeared in print Sokal revealed that it was a hoax.[26]
He had written the paper with an extensive bibliography that
included all the chic names, using lots of technical terminology,

alongside jargon-laden phrases like "problematized" and "relativized" in support of a theory that anyone with common sense would have seen was untenable.

By using similar techniques of argument, although of course without any hint of parody, Bernal in *Black Athena* was able to dispense with the disciplines of linguistics and philology on the grounds that they were implicated in European racial politics. Of course it was easier for most people to recognize the nonsensical nature of the assertions in Sokal's bogus paper than it was to understand why it was extremely unlikely that philosophy had its origins in a fictional Egyptian Mystery System. In science new data will always be available to test and retest theories. You need only to jump out of a window to discover whether or not gravity works.[27]

Arming America, a book published in 2000 but based on work begun in the 1990s, provides an instructive parallel to *Black Athena* and the ethical limbo which made its assertions seem tenable.[28] Michael Bellesiles, then a professor at Emory University, was rightly critical of narratives written about the history of the United States that paid little or no attention to women and minorities. His book challenged the deeply held (but untested) presumption that early Americans ordinarily possessed firearms, as was apparently suggested by the Second Amendment to the Constitution, added in 1791, which provided that "the right of the people to keep and bear arms shall not be infringed."

If Bellesiles could have shown that in reality firearms had been a relative rarity, he would have been able to undermine the major historical arguments that have been used against gun control. *Arming America* was full of detailed charts, data, and footnotes that appeared to support his case that in the eighteenth and nineteenth centuries it was unusual for ordinary citizens to own guns. The range of materials, times, and places considered was broad.

According to Peter Charles Hoffer, the strategy Bellesiles employed was:

> Dazzle the reader with erudition and hammer the opposition with arguments. When conservative critics raise questions about the veracity of the research and the validity of the conclusions, accuse them of lacking expertise and exhibiting an excess of partisanship. When fellow professionals begin to raise similar questions about the work, claim that the NRA [National Rifle Association] and its stooges are out to get him.[29]

Similar strategies had worked well also for Bernal in the controversy over his theories. In the opening pages of *Black Athena* he presented discussions of orthographies of various ancient languages, followed by tables and maps. He covered an unusually wide range of materials in the book, and with quotations from several different ancient languages, in their distinctive scripts. The bibliography was extensive.

In 1996 Bellesiles published an article in the *Journal of American History* stating the main lines of the argument he would later make in the book, but without supplying all the necessary supporting evidence. There were elementary methodological problems in his research, including incorrectly calculated percentages. The tables did not indicate clearly where his data had come from.

Why had the journal allowed the article to be published? In the article, Bellesiles thanked David Thelen, the editor, for his "enthusiasm." As Hoffer observes, "overturning received wisdom on a subject of such historical and present-day importance was a sure-fire attention getter for Thelen."[30] When a graduate student had raised questions about the published article, Bellesiles, without trying to refute him, sought to discredit him on personal grounds "as a gun nut and a crank" because of his known association with the NRA.[31]

Still, when scholars began to look at the data presented in the article, and then later in greater detail in the book, problems began to emerge. Some critics brushed aside the inconsistencies and miscalculations, arguing that it was inevitable for some mistakes to be made in a work with such a wide sweep and high-minded purpose. In 2001 the book won Columbia University's Bancroft Prize for the most distinguished work in American history.[32]

Nonetheless, enough questions had been raised by scholars for the History Department at Emory to arrange a formal investigation by an outside committee of experts. After three months of inquiry, the committee found that Bellesiles' research was flawed and that he had often deviated from accepted practice. In the construction of a table of data vital to his case, they found "evidence of falsification."[33] In December 2002 Columbia University rescinded the Bancroft Prize. Bellesiles did not admit that he had done wrong, but he resigned from his position at Emory. He still has his defenders, who believe that such mistakes as he made did not damage his case, and that pressure from the NRA and gun enthusiasts was in large measure responsible for his being discredited. He published a revised edition of the book in 2003.[34]

Like *Arming America, Black Athena* presented exciting new narratives that promised to overturn the way history had been written. In both cases scholars were prepared to accept their findings with enthusiasm, and without close investigation of the supporting data they presented. *Black Athena* was indeed published by a university press (Rutgers), but under somewhat anomalous circumstances.[35] First published in England by Free Association Books, the first volume of *Black Athena* was turned down by professional reviewers for several different university presses in the United States. The director of Rutgers University Press, however, accepted the project as one of the three books that he had authority to publish in 1987 without going through the usual reviewing process.

Bellesiles refuses to admit that he deliberately intended to misrepresent the data. I have no reason to suppose that Bernal did anything other than describe what he was prepared to see, but even if Bernal did not intend to distort the evidence, the net result of his efforts is the same as if he did. So a response was necessary, not just because of the underlying ethical issues of fairness to the evidence, as well as to other scholars whose motives he has misrepresented or misreported, and whose integrity he has questioned. Knowing how he had misrepresented the views of earlier classical scholars, I had little reason to hope that he would be kinder to me and those who supported me. It should go without saying that he was prepared to believe that we were all driven by traditionalism and political conservatism.

The Dutch ancient historian Josine Blok openly confronted

this issue in her assessment of Bernal's work: "In the writing of history, fairness of argument and decency in proof are equally indispensable."[36] It is beyond the pale and indeed unprofessional in scholarship to attribute motives to others that they may not have had, or to misrepresent what they have said, or to put words into their mouths. What excuse did Bernal have for mentioning only the most pejorative of a number of possible explanations, such as racism? Why insist on racism as the explanation for the change in attitude toward Egyptian influence, when it was completely evident that what transformed history was the decipherment of hieroglyphics?

"Decency in proof" means that one cannot substitute plausibility for fact. In effect, the appeal to plausibility is a complex way of saying that facts do not matter, which is essentially the same argument that Selwyn Cudjoe used against me in the debate about *Not Out of Africa*.

The historian who relies on facts is usually reluctant to make leaps of faith. He or she would assume that Cleopatra considered herself a Macedonian Greek, like her ancestors, even though her father's mother might not have been a Macedonian Greek (which doesn't necessarily mean that this unknown female was Egyptian or Nubian or Jewish or Persian, just as it does not entirely exclude those possibilities). By contrast, a writer who prefers to argue on the basis of plausibilities begins from the premise that authenticity can be determined only subjectively. If there is a possibility, no matter how remote, that Cleopatra *might* have been black, then it seems plausible to the cultural historian who resorts to this type of reasoning to conclude that she *was* black.

If the idea of a black Cleopatra seems plausible to you, try this test. How plausible is it to you that Cleopatra was Jewish?[37] Your skepticism is surely justified, but the claim that she was Jewish has exactly the same factual basis as the claim that she was black, namely, silence and possibility: we do not know the identity of her paternal grandmother. Since no ancient historian says anything about this woman, the most likely possibility is that she was a Macedonian Greek, like the other members of the royal family. The only reason to suppose that she was black is that in the slave-owning American South, white men sometimes had black mistresses. That argument has resonance for us today, but in antiquity slaves came in all colors and nationalities.

Narratives based on plausibility or desirability have their uses, and can be instructive and illuminating, but they bear a closer resemblance to myth than they do to history. Of course we may never know all that we would like to know about Cleopatra's grandmother or about many more important aspects of ancient history. A narrative that takes account of the known facts about Egypt and Greece will most likely serve no modern social needs whatever, and be not nearly so interesting or revolutionary as one that we could design to please ourselves.

Epilogue

Was it worth it? Yes, even if it meant being a defendant in a lawsuit and listening to people say some pretty unkind things about me. In a way, it was rather fun collecting nasty epithets. My favorite is Wilson Moses' "obscure drudge in the academic backwaters of a classics department."[1] Why throw in the whole field of classical studies? Maybe he didn't like his high-school Latin teacher.

But in spite of all that, I learned so much, not just about the Stolen Legacy myth and its origins, but about African-American history, and history generally. Even with all the anguish and worry that was involved, it was a privilege to be involved in an important intellectual controversy, to need to explain myself, and to take nothing for granted. In the end, I think I managed to convince quite a few people that myth shouldn't be taught as history. I met some wonderful people who I never would have encountered if I'd kept my eyes firmly fixed on the ancient world.

I even won some recognition for my work, in the form of awards and even honorary degrees. In 1996, around the time that Selwyn Cudjoe was accusing me of Eurocentrism and goodness knows what else, Trinity College in Hartford understood what I was trying to do.[2] The citation for the doctorate of humane letters the college awarded me said in part: "Out of your deep concern for intellectual integrity in higher education, you remind us that to be credible we must ask hard questions and address controversial issues forthrightly."

Asking hard questions is what educational institutions ought to be doing, because they provide a great opportunity for learning. But we need to present issues so that students can make use of scholarly values and arrive at independent judgments about controversial issues. I have seen how it can be done so that everyone benefits.

In fall 2002 a former colleague invited me to give a talk about *Not Out of Africa* at Lehigh University, where he was now the chairman of Afro-American Studies. I hadn't heard from Bill Scott in decades, since he left Wellesley for Oberlin some thirty years earlier. I had known Scott well when he was on our campus and was starting to build up Wellesley's Black Studies Department. He left Wellesley not long after Tony Martin got tenure.

Scott knew all about the controversy over *Not Out of Africa*, and that was why he had invited me to give a public lecture and talk to his seminar. A well-known Afrocentrist was coming to speak to the class later in the semester. Students could hear both sides and make up their own minds.

Scott also wanted me to meet with faculty colleagues and graduate students. In the event, there were some serious disagreements and some tough discussions, but in an atmosphere of cordiality and civility. Scott had set the tone: The idea was to talk about evidence, and how we know what we know. People were there to listen and learn and discuss. Blacks and whites were listening to one another. Whites were learning about black experience and making it part of their own lives, which is what ought to happen.

Every campus should be able to offer that kind of atmosphere for discussion. I have been asked to speak in formats that allow for debate because *Not Out of Africa* has been regarded as controversial, and orderly dialogue is a productive way to identify and address areas of misunderstanding. Usually we kept on talking long after the main presentation was over.

I can testify that I have learned from commentators and responders to my talks on different campuses. They made me realize that I should have made an effort to talk with more people before I wrote *Not Out of Africa*. If I had done so, and not simply sought to debunk myths that were being taught as history, I would have realized that the myth of the Stolen Legacy had great symbolic value.[3] I simply had not realized how many people grew up believing in or imagining there was some truth in the stories about the Egyptian origins of Greek philosophy.

The positive side of the notion of a Stolen Legacy is that it states clearly that Africa and its people played an important role in world history, as it has, since it seems certain that the human race originated in Africa. It would have been more effective to discuss and acknowledge the symbolic meaning of these myths before I tried to set out all the reasons why it would be better for all of us not literally to believe in these stories.

But my failure sufficiently to take into account people's feelings was not a valid justification for the kind of rhetoric my book provoked. The name-calling and false assertions about my motives belong to the world of politics. In academe, the right way to respond to someone who you think is wrong is by reasoned argument, explanation, and information, especially since our common goal is to educate young people and, while we are at it, ourselves.

People who are unwilling to listen and learn should have no place in academe, but of course they are well entrenched there, as we have seen. For their proponents, the myths of the Stolen Legacy and Jewish responsibility for the slave trade are hallowed truths, not to mention a fruitful source of extra income. The faculty who teach these myths as truth will not have their minds changed by anything that I have said or written. To defend their views, all they need to do is to claim that their critics are racists, and someone is certain to listen.

Dr. Y. A. A. ben-Jochannan has continued to say what he has always said about Greek philosophy being stolen from Egypt.[4] He is still advising people to read books that were written before the decipherment of hieroglyphics, because those books say what he wants them to hear.

Tony Martin, in an encyclopedia article about Black Studies at Wellesley, still talks about a "Jewish onslaught." This latest narrative, published in 2005, makes me sound even more sinister than I did in the various "Broadsides" that he published during the 1990s.[5] Now, it seems, I "heckled" ben-Jochannan, although all I did was ask for clarification in the question period after the lecture. It was I, Martin claims, and not my colleague who "summoned" a student to my office and "harangued [her] for a considerable period" about Cleopatra, and so on. There is only one hero in the story, Martin himself.

Martin concluded that Black Studies at Wellesley exists "within a constant aura of siege": "In many ways the story of Black Studies may simply be the story of being black in America—writ small." If only it were true that the story of being black in America were like the story of being a tenured professor in the Africana Studies Department at Wellesley, with all the perquisites and job security that such faculty members enjoy! "Nice work if you can get it—and skilled race pros certainly do," says Jim Sleeper.

As Sleeper has also observed, academics like Martin need to define blackness in oppositional terms, because they derive their power and significance from the idea that they are excluded from society:

> Playing this game involves finding racism in every leaf that falls while relying on reservoirs of white racial guilt and deference whose existence black racists deny even as they accept media pulpits, book royalties, academic tenure, and constitutional protections.[6]

But despite the reality of the privileged positions that they enjoy, race professionals insist that they are mistreated. The strategy, which John McWhorter calls "therapeutic alienation," requires them to maintain that they are victims of a depraved oppression.[7]

Martin's article appears in the *Encyclopedia of Black Studies,* a volume that will be used as a standard reference book in many libraries. It is certainly possible that some readers will be able to see that the account is too narrowly focused on the experience of its author. Still, many young students may be led to believe that Jews are the enemies of Black Studies and to accept much else in the account that seems to me, as a witness to the same events, to be at variance with the evidence.

Alternative narratives like Martin's encyclopedia article will continue to carry conviction, at least with some people, and academics will continue to defend them as "truths" by refusing to see that by truth they mean opinion. They may even persuade themselves that there can be many truths, and that all can be of equal value. Or they may insist that they cannot make any judgment, even when the issues are clear-cut. As a Wellesley professor said to me about the question of Aristotle stealing his philosophy, "I couldn't take sides because it wasn't my field." But there is no good reason why she couldn't have sought to inform herself. Except perhaps for the issue of race, and the idea that she might have been doing some social good by withholding judgment.

Perhaps we can see our situation more clearly if we look at the ethnic tensions raised by scholarship in a field unconnected with the racial politics of this country. In recent years Hindu nationalists have criticized the non-Indian scholars of Hindu culture for their lax morals. They insist that only Indians can understand Hindu culture. Nationalists have also sent death threats to an Indian scholar, because his work has shown that Hindus in the past were prepared to eat beef.[8]

By their hostility to historians who derive their conclusions from evidence, the Hindu right has had a "chilling effect" on other areas of scholarship as well, such as art history and archaeology.[9] In its stead, Martha Nussbaum suggests a new etiquette for scholars working on sensitive issues, with some general guidelines. Scholars need to show respect for minority points of view and to be sure their approach does not marginalize the contribution of any group. On the other hand, scholars should not be afraid to say something because it will embarrass other people, even if they are members of an oppressed minority. No one should assume that only "an insider," such as a member of an ethnic minority, is automatically qualified to write or teach about that ethnic group: "there is no reason to suppose that birth within a culture automatically confers understanding."[10]

Whether in the case of the history of India or of ancient Africa, the solution is not to argue that all narratives are political, and that therefore there is no such thing as truth. Rather, the narrative that educators should choose "must square itself with the data—textual, documentary, archaeological—and if there are parts that won't square, one must be truthful about them."[11] In order to confront racism in this country, black and white educators alike must "build colleges and universities that conquer racism by thought and brain and plan, by the dissemination of truth and the demolition of pernicious myths and stereotypes." As Nussbaum reminds us, being more inclusive, and more sensitive to ethnic and social issues, does not require us to jettison "sound scholarly values."

We now need to ask what happens if we take on the responsibility of deciding among the various narratives, and demonstrate that some are supported by better evidence than others, and that some are even demonstrably false. Educators who teach contrafactual narratives will appeal to the doctrine of academic freedom, which they will interpret to mean that anyone can say anything. But academic freedom was designed to allow faculty members to express opinions or discuss theories that are controversial. It was not intended to protect individuals like Holocaust deniers who seek to teach what is demonstrably false.[12]

In practice there are established limits to academic freedom. As we have seen, Michael Bellesiles resigned when a group of experts found that his conclusions were based on nonexistent or unverifiable data.[13] Scientists who falsify data in order to get research grants are disciplined. Why shouldn't similar scrutiny be applied to people who teach or indeed write demonstrably false statements about history and simply ignore the evidence when it is presented to them? This is a profound breach of ethical duty for any scholar.

Under the rules in effect at most universities, the faculties and administrations have the power annually to review all courses in the curriculum. Usually only new courses receive close scrutiny. Yet there is constant change in the quality and content even of established courses. We typically do not choose to intervene in those because we trust our colleagues. The system works and has worked in the overwhelming majority of cases. In those rare instances when professors do not police themselves, we normally throw up our hands in despair and frustration and say we can't do anything about it.

But how ethical is it to abandon responsibility for what is being taught? Do we really believe that students who are taught what is manifestly untrue will not be seriously harmed? Certainly in most cases they will suffer no physical damage. But their ability to reason will hardly be enhanced by the teaching of nonsense and falsehoods, and at least some of those students will be prepared to believe that instructors who are in fact better informed are *lying* to them. I know. I have seen it in action. At a meeting of the Wellesley student senate in March 1993, one student observed about *The Secret Relationship Between Blacks and Jews:* "I took the class that read it last semester, from what I read it was not anti-semitic. The work was well footnoted . . ."[14]

Too often we try to defend the teaching of hatred by pointing out that racist texts have been used over the years in many classes taught by white professors. That may be true, but by now everyone has been made keenly aware of the failure of past scholars to pay attention to minorities and women, and most educators today make a genuine effort to avoid that wrong. Even if there are some professors who still cling to such outmoded ways of thinking, their shortcomings would not provide a justification for the uncritical use of a book like *The Secret Relationship.* Two wrongs do not make a right.

Wherever racism of any sort exists we should object strenuously. We also need to recognize that there are other racisms than white against black. If a dean can reprimand a professor for "hindering diversity" because he said that the Holocaust was unique in history, he or she can certainly ask another professor why he insists on teaching that Jews are responsible for the slave trade.[15] But the issue in either case is not whether or not these remarks were hurtful to some people. The question is whether the professors' claims are based on sound research and warranted evidence.

Speaking out and writing about these issues, as some of us have done, is an important first step. But academics need to express disapproval in more direct ways, or we will be delinquent in our responsibilities as educators. Limiting or docking salaries is one possibility. Another is denying approval for particular requirements, as when Wellesley's History Department refused to give credit toward a history major for courses in the Africana Studies Department. Departments also have the power to decide what courses will be offered. They should be the front line of defense of scholarly values, because they have the best knowledge of their particular fields.

People outside academia may wonder why I do not recommend more stringent methods than these—such as revoking a professor's tenure—but under university regulations these are the only ways open to us. According to the articles of government at Wellesley, tenure can be broken if a faculty member commits an act of "proved moral delinquency," such as a felony, or has a physical or mental disability that impairs his or her power to teach. The other causes listed are less easily defined: failure to maintain high standards in teaching and serious failure to cooperate with the department or the college. In practice, legal counsel would probably advise taking action only if the faculty member in question regularly failed to turn up for class. They would not recommend making judgments about quality of instruction, because these would inevitably lead to costly and divisive litigation.

In addition, when judging quality of instruction universities need to go out of their way to protect academic freedom. Otherwise they will be subject to constant pressure from outside groups to remove faculty whose views were offensive to them. Tenure has been the only sure guarantee of the academic freedom to try out new ideas and to question established beliefs. People have often asked me, "Is that guy [Tony Martin] still at Wellesley?" Until he retired in 2007, my answer was, where else would he be?

On the other hand, I do not believe that we should continue to permit the doctrine of academic freedom to serve as a protective smokescreen for the kind of discourse that has no place in a university. Hate speech and hate literature like *The Secret Relationship* have worked their way into academe from the world of politics. The aim of hate speech is to incite to action, to persuade quickly and win, rather than to reflect and uncover the truth. But once the first ethnic slur is made, or the first political insult, serious debate about historical accuracy becomes almost impossible.

To make any progress, we need to be vigilant and decisive. In 2003 Wellesley did the right thing in refusing to pay the honorarium for an event featuring the poet Amiri Baraka. Supposedly the purpose of the event was to hold a serious discussion about academic freedom. But to judge from what Baraka had reportedly done on other campuses, almost certainly it would have been the occasion for a solidarity rally, with Jews once again chosen as the common enemy. In 1993 no one would have dared to say anything about the proposal.

Amiri Baraka, formerly Leroi Jones, is a well-known protest playwright and poet. At the time Baraka had been in the news because in his poem "Somebody Blew Up America" he had said that Jews (including Ariel Sharon, then the prime minister of

Israel) had deliberately stayed away from the World Trade Center in New York on September 11, 2001, because they knew in advance that the towers would be destroyed.[16] There was no truth to these allegations. They were based on propaganda circulated in Arab media after the terrorist attacks.[17]

Perhaps some of the students who proposed the lecture didn't know exactly who Baraka was, or had been encouraged to invite him by someone or some group who didn't tell them the whole story. But as soon as the administration and faculty explained what Baraka had been doing elsewhere, other black students and Jewish students began working together. Jewish students organized a protest on the day of the lecture. They were joined by a large and diverse group of students, faculty, staff, and townspeople. The large audience included black people who had been on the picket line and white people (including Jews) who had not participated in the protest.

Some black students gave Baraka a standing ovation when he read his poem. Other students left the auditorium, some in tears, when Baraka expressed his views about Israel, calling it a "neofascist nation."[18] People in the audience shouted "Liar!" when he said that no Israelis died in the World Trade Center. Baraka asked for proof. But of course the names of the six Israelis among the victims had long since been recorded.[19]

Without question, Baraka's poem "Somebody Blew Up America" made some valid points about everyone's responsibility for the wrongs done in our society, but many students weren't able to hear that message because they were so angry at the demonstrably false allegations that Baraka had been making about Israelis and Jews. His aggressive tactics and provocative statements distracted many members of his audience from what might otherwise have been an occasion for serious self-examination.

Nonetheless we had made progress. Despite the angry exchanges with Baraka, students tended to treat one another with respect. When the leader of the black student organization Nubian saw the protest outside the lecture hall, she said: "I was like, right on . . . ," "These are some of my good friends . . . All we can do is learn from each other."

But that progress would not have happened if President Walsh and members of the faculty and administration had not stated their disapproval and made the moral judgment not to pay Baraka a large honorarium.[20] We cannot protect students from hate speech, which they can hear all around them and read on the Internet. But we can and should take every opportunity we have to condemn hate speakers and to see that they are not generously rewarded.

It is of course much easier to make such decisions about outside lecturers than it is about tenured faculty. What if they teach hatred only ten percent of the time? How much is too much? In practice, universities have refused even to ask questions. But both faculty and students would be better served (and educated) by open discussion.

Moral decisions are not always easy to make, as this book has shown. They can make your life difficult, especially when you fail to get support from the very colleagues and administrators who should have been standing by your side. But I like to think that, if the question came up again today, some people might take my concerns about the ethics of teaching manifest falsehood more seriously than they were prepared to do back in 1992.

Notes

Introduction

1. On the theory that no historical narrative can be authoritative, see esp. Alan B. Spitzer, *Historical Truth and Lies About the Past* (Chapel Hill: University of North Carolina Press, 1996), pp. 2–3. On postmodernist approaches to reality, see Barbara S. Held, *Psychology's Interpretive Turn* (Washington: American Psychological Association, 2007), pp. 28–32.

2. On the limitations of "consensus" history, see esp. Peter Charles Hoffer, *Past Imperfect: Facts, Fictions, and Fraud in the Writing of American History* (New York: Basic Books, 2004), pp. 59–60; Richard J. Evans, *In Defense of History* (New York: W. W. Norton, 1999), pp. 210–16.

3. On Elisabeth Burgos-Debray, ed., *I, Rigoberta Menchú: An Indian Woman in Guatemala*, tr. Ann Wright (New York: Verso, 1998), see esp. David Stoll, *Rigoberta Menchú and the Story of All Poor Guatemalans* (Boulder: Westview Press, 1999) pp. ix–xiii, and Larry Rohter, "Tarnished Laureate," in *The Rigoberta Menchú Controversy* (Minneapolis: University of Minnesota Press, 2001), pp. 58–65.

4. James Frey, *A Million Little Pieces* (New York: Doubleday, 2005); Edward Wyatt, "Live on 'Oprah,' a Memoirist Is Kicked Out of the Book Club," *New York Times,* 27 January 2006.

5. George G. M. James, *Stolen Legacy* (New York: Philosophical Library, 1954).

6. Mary Lefkowitz, *Not Out of Africa: How Afrocentrism Became an Excuse to Teach Myth as History* (New York: Basic Books, 1996, 1997).

7. Donald Alexander Downs, *Cornell '69: Liberalism and the Crisis of the American University* (Ithaca: Cornell University Press, 1999), p. 308.

ONE
A Racist Incident?

1. Sunita Subramanian, Julie Provost, and Jennifer J. Paull, "Interviews with Professor Anthony Martin and Student Michelle Plantec," *Galenstone,* issue 5 (May 1993), p. 8. My account of the incident closely follows the text of these interviews as reported in this article, pp. 8–10.
2. Ibid., p. 8.
3. Ibid., p. 8.
4. Ibid., p. 9.
5. Ibid., p. 9.
6. Ibid., p. 10.
7. Ibid., p. 8.
8. Ibid., p. 10.
9. Michelle Plantec, Letter to Ms. [Emily] Tobin of the American Civil Liberties Union (ACLU), 8 March 1992.
10. Subramanian, Provost, and Paull, "Interviews," p. 9.
11. Ibid., p. 10.
12. Ibid., p. 9.
13. Nannerl O. Keohane, Letter to Tony Martin, 20 March 1992.
14. Subramanian, Provost, and Paull, "Interviews," p. 8.
15. A notorious incident involving an African-American male occurred in fall 1990. The Boston Celtics' top draft choice Dee Brown was ordered out of his car by the Town of Wellesley Police, told to drop his gun (he was holding a pen), and commanded to lie on the ground with his hands behind his back. The police had mistaken him for a bank robber; see Peter May and Jerry Thomas, "Officers Hold Celtic at Gunpoint," *Boston Globe,* 22 September 1990, Metro p. 1.
16. Alan Charles Kors and Harvey A. Silverglate, *The Shadow University: The Betrayal of Liberty on America's Campuses* (New York: Free Press, 1998), pp. 9–33; Neil Hamilton, *Zealotry and Academic Freedom* (New Brunswick: Transaction Publishers, 1995), p. 118 n. 142.

17. Ibid., p. 9.

18. Ibid., pp. 32–33. For a detailed account, see Donald Alexander Downs, *Restoring Free Speech and Liberty on Campus* (Cambridge: Independent Institute/Cambridge University Press, 2005), pp. 168–89.

19. On the importance of the intervention by Kors, see ibid., pp. 265–67.

20. Ironically, in academe, race and culture are now less serious problems than economic inequality; see Walter Benn Michaels, *The Trouble with Diversity: How We Learned to Love Identity and Ignore Inequality* (New York: Metropolitan Books, 2006).

T W O
Discovering Afrocentrism

1. Martin Bernal, *Black Athena: The Afroasiatic Roots of Classical Civilization,* vol. 1: *The Fabrication of Ancient Greece* (Rutgers, N.J.: Rutgers University Press, 1987), and vol. 2: *The Archaeological and Documentary Evidence* (Rutgers, N.J.: Rutgers University Press, 1991); these volumes are hereafter cited as *BA* I and *BA* II, respectively.

2. *BA* I, pp. 51–52. On why the etymology Neith/Athena is invalid, see Jay H. Jasanoff and Alan Nussbaum, "Word Games: The Linguistic Evidence in *Black Athena,*" in *Black Athena Revisited,* ed. Mary R. Lefkowitz and Guy MacLean Rogers (Chapel Hill: University of North Carolina Press, 1996), pp. 193–94. In *Black Athena,* vol. 3: *The Linguistic Evidence* (New Brunswick, N.J.: Rutgers University Press, 2006), p. 548, Bernal claims that the title was inspired by a representation of the head of Athena on a silver coin, "portrayed . . . in such a way that she could be taken as an African black." But thick lips and globular eyes (ibid., p. 686, n. 42) are not exclusively black characteristics, and no other coin portraits of Athena have such features. In the early 1990s Bernal sought to support Afrocentric

claims that Socrates was black on the grounds that his face on a fourth-century statue has a snub nose and wide mouth. But those features also are not exclusively black, and in any case, that particular characterization of Socrates was based on an imaginative portrayal of Socrates in Plato's *Symposium*, not on life; see Mary Lefkowitz, *Not Out of Africa: How Afrocentrism Became an Excuse to Teach Myth as History* (New York: Basic Books, 1996, 1997), pp. 29–30.

3. George G. M. James, *Stolen Legacy* (New York: Philosophical Library, 1954); Y. A. A. ben-Jochannan, *Africa: Mother of Western Civilization* (Baltimore: Black Classic Press, 1988 [1971]).

4. *BA* I, p. 38.

5. National Black United Front, "Dr. Yosef A. A. ben-Jochannan: Curriculum Vitae," www.nbufront.org/html/MastersMuseums/DocBen/BioInfo.html.

6. *BA* I, p. 71.

7. Edward Said, *Orientalism* (New York: Vintage, 1978).

8. *BA* I, p. 242.

9. *BA* II, p. 5.

10. Michel Foucault, *Madness and Civilization* (London: Tavistock, 1967), translated from *Histoire de la Folie à l'Âge Classique* (1961).

11. Mary R. Lefkowitz, *The Lives of the Greek Poets* (Baltimore: Johns Hopkins University Press, 1981).

12. *BA* I, p. 3.

13. Mary Lefkowitz, "Not Out of Africa: The Origins of Greece and the Illusions of Afrocentrists," *New Republic,* 10 February 1992, pp. 29–36; reprinted (with revisions) as "Ancient History: Modern Myths" in *Black Athena Revisited,* ed. Mary R. Lefkowitz and Guy MacLean Rogers (Chapel Hill: University of North Carolina Press, 1996), pp. 3–23.

14. Marcus Garvey, as quoted in *Negro Social and Political Thought, 1850–1920: Representative Texts,* ed. Howard Brotz (New York: Basic Books, 1966), pp. 561–62; see Lefkowitz, *Not Out of Africa,* pp. 130–34.

15. On Diop, see Lefkowitz, *Not Out of Africa,* pp. 151–53, and in general François-Xavier Fauvelle-Aymar, "Cheikh Anta Diop, ou l'Africaniste Malgré Lui," in *Afrocentrismes,* ed. François-Xavier Fauvelle-Aymar, Jean-Pierre Chrétien, and Claude-Hélène Perrot (Paris: Karthala, 2000), pp. 27–46.

16. Amy J. Binder, *Contentious Curricula: Afrocentrism and Creationism in American Public Schools* (Princeton: Princeton University Press, 2002), p. 34.

17. Nicholas Wade, *Before the Dawn: Recovering the Lost History of Our Ancestors* (New York: Penguin Books, 2006), pp. 181–201.

18. Donald B. Redford, *From Slave to Pharaoh: The Black Experience of Ancient Egypt* (Baltimore: Johns Hopkins University Press, 2004), pp. 5–6.

19. See Roger D. Woodard, "Attic Greek," in *The Cambridge Encyclopedia of Ancient Languages,* ed. Roger D. Woodard (Cambridge: Cambridge University Press, 2004), p. 648.

20. Manfred Bietak, *Avaris: The Capital of the Hyksos; Recent Excavations at Tell el Dab'a* (London: British Museum Press 1996), p. 81.

21. For more details, see Stanley M. Burstein, "A Contested History: Egypt, Greece, and Afrocentrism," in *Current Issues and the Study of Ancient History,* by Stanley M. Burstein et al. (Publications of the Association of Ancient Historians 7; Claremont: Regina Books, 2002), pp. 25–29.

22. Walter Burkert, *Babylon, Memphis, Persepolis: Eastern Contexts of Greek Culture* (Cambridge: Harvard University Press, 2005), pp. 72–74.

23. Ibid.; see also Alfred Wiedemann, *Sammlung Altägyptischer Wörter von klassischen Autoren umschrieben oder übersetzt worden sind* (Leipzig: Johann Ambrosius Barth, 1883), p. 17.

24. Stephanie Dalley and A. T. Reyes, "Mesopotamian Contact and Influence in the Greek World (1)," in *The Legacy of Mesopotamia* (Oxford: Clarendon Press, 1998), p. 104; G. J. Toomer, "Mathematics

and Astronomy," in *Legacy of Egypt,* ed. J. R. Harris (Oxford: Clarendon Press, 1971), pp. 44–45; see also Palter, "*Black Athena,* Afrocentrism, and the History of Science," pp. 216, 255–56.

25. Richard J. Gillings, *Mathematics in the Time of Pharaohs* (New York: Dover Publications, 1971), pp. 233–34.

26. Lionel Casson, *Libraries in the Ancient World* (New Haven: Yale University Press, 2001), pp. 32–33.

27. Richard Jasnow and Karl-Theodor Zauzich, *The Ancient Egyptian Book of Thoth* (Wiesbaden: Harrasowitz Verlag, 2005), pp. 65–71.

28. Ibid., p. 71.

29. *Corpus Hermeticum* 2.12; Brian P. Copenhaver, *Hermetica* (Cambridge: Cambridge University Press, 1992), p. 11.

THREE
Two Views of Ancient History

1. On the emphasis on color, see esp. Jim Sleeper, *Liberal Racism* (New York: Viking, 1997), p. 96.

2. Precise statistics about Africans in ancient Europe are unavailable; see F. M. Snowden, Jr., *Blacks in Antiquity* (Cambridge: Harvard University Press, 1970), p. 183. Some were servants or slaves; ibid., p. 323 n. 98 and p. 184, and also Balbina Baebler, *Fleissige Thrakerinnen und wehrhafte Skythen* (Leipzig: B. G. Teubner 1998), p. 74.

3. Jerold Auerbach, "Anti-Semitism at Wellesley College," *Congress Monthly,* July–August 1993, p. 10.

4. Alice Dembner, "Wellesley Denies Raise to Professor," *Boston Globe,* 26 August 1994, pp. A23, 28; Julie L. Nicklin, "Wellesley Professor Fails to Prove Libel Against Student," *Chronicle of Higher Education,* 15 January 1999, p. A16.

5. Tony Martin, memo to Mary Lefkowitz, 23 April 1992.

6. Nalida Lacet and Kamillah Yasin, " 'Africans in Antiquity' course addresses 'The Illusions of Eurocentrism,' " *Wellesley News,* 10 May 1992, p. 10.

7. In 1994 Martin began an interview with a reporter from the *Boston Globe* by asking if she was Jewish; see Irene Sege, "Teaching History or Hate," *Boston Globe,* 24 February 1994, Living p. 51.

8. Mary Lefkowitz, "Lefkowitz Defends Stance on Afro-Asiatic Origins of Greek Culture," *Wellesley News,* 10 May 1992, p. 10.

9. Orlando Patterson, *Freedom in the Making of Western Culture* (New York: Basic Books, 1991).

10. Mary Lefkowitz, "Afrocentrism Poses a Threat to the Rationalist Tradition," *Chronicle of Higher Education,* 6 May 1992, p. A52.

11. Tony Martin and his two students were quoting from Aubrey de Sélincourt, trans., *Herodotus: The Histories* (Baltimore: Penguin Books, 1972). De Sélincourt (p. 146) translates: "both the parents of Heracles . . . were of Egyptian origin"; the Greek says "descended from Aegyptus" (2.43.2), who was in fact of Greek descent; see Mary Lefkowitz, *Not Out of Africa: How Afrocentrism Became an Excuse to Teach Myth as History* (New York: Basic Books, 1997), pp. 199–200, 242–43. De Sélincourt (p. 178) translates: "doctrine of the immortality of the soul"; the Greek says: "tell this story (*logos*), that the soul is deathless" (2.123.2), Lefkowitz, *Not Out of Africa,* p. 68.

12. Judith Martin and Gunther S. Stent, "I Think; Therefore I Thank," *American Scholar,* 59, no. 2 (1990), 237–54.

13. Mary Lynn F. Jones, "Afrocentrism Debate Continues," *Wellesley News,* 7 October 1992, pp. 1, 4.

FOUR

Turning Myths into History

1. Mia Bay, *The White Image in the Black Mind: African-American Ideas About White People, 1830–1925* (New York: Oxford University Press, 2000), p. 212.

2. Clinton M. Jean, *Behind the Eurocentric Veils: The Search for African Realities* (Amherst: University of Massachusetts Press, 1991).

3. Ibid., pp. 97–99. See also the review of Jean's book by Kwame

Anthony Appiah, *Times Literary Supplement,* 12 February 1993, pp. 24–35.

4. Plato, *Republic* 414b9.

5. Jean, *Behind the Eurocentric Veils,* pp. 58–59.

6. Harold Brackman, *Ministry of Lies: The Truth Behind the Nation of Islam's "The Secret Relationship Between Blacks and Jews"* (New York: Four Walls, Eight Windows, 1994), p. 105.

7. Murray Friedman, *What Went Wrong: The Creation and Collapse of the Black-Jewish Alliance* (New York: Free Press, 1995), p. 59; Andrew Hacker, "Jewish Racism, Black Anti-Semitism," in *Blacks and Jews,* ed. Paul Berman (New York: Delacorte Press, 1994), p. 162.

8. Historical Research Department of the Nation of Islam, *The Secret Relationship Between Blacks and Jews,* vol. 1 (Chicago: The Nation of Islam, 1991).

9. Both quotations from ibid., p. vii.

10. Brackman, *Ministry of Lies,* p. 25.

11. See esp. Goran Larsson, *Fact or Fraud: The Protocols of the Elders of Zion* (San Diego: Jerusalem Center for Biblical Studies and Research, 1994), pp. 15–21.

12. Ibid., 34–35.

13. Brackman, *Ministry of Lies,* pp. 45–60.

14. Ibid., pp. 61–89; see also Nat Trager, *Empire of Hate* (Fort Lauderdale: Coral Reef Books), pp. 27–75; Daniel Pipes, *Conspiracy: How the Paranoid Style Flourishes and Where It Comes From* (New York: Free Press, 1997), pp. 5–6. The charges against Jews made in *The Secret Relationship* were condemned in a statement by the American Historical Association; Karen J. Winkler, "Group Issues Statement on Role of Jews in Slave Trade," *Chronicle of Higher Education,* 17 February 1995.

15. Hugh Thomas, *The Slave Trade* (New York: Simon and Schuster, 1997), p. 12.

16. Eli Faber, *Jews, Slaves, and the Slave Trade: Setting the Record Straight* (New York: New York University Press, 1998), p. 145.

17. Trager, *Empire of Hate,* pp. 106–7.

18. Thomas, *The Slave Trade,* p. 804.

19. Trager, *Empire of Hate,* pp. 109–27. See also Steven A. Holmes, "Slavery Is an Issue Again," *New York Times,* 24 March 1996; Colin Nickerson, "One by One, Slaves in Sudan Are Bought and Freed by Western Groups; Why Does the UN Deplore the Practice?" *Boston Globe Magazine,* 19 December 1999, p. 15; Marc Lacey, "Panel Led by U.S. Criticizes Sudan's Government over Slavery," *New York Times,* 23 May 2002.

20. Alan Charles Kors and Harvey A. Silverglate, *The Shadow University* (New York: Free Press, 1998), p. 134. For the full text of the speech see www.feastofhateandfear.com/archives/jeffries.html.

21. Henry Louis Gates, Jr., "Black Demagogues and Pseudo-Scholars," *New York Times,* 20 July 1992, p. A15.

22. On the difficulties involved even in *discussing* the issue of reparations, see David Horowitz, *Uncivil Wars: The Controversy over Reparations for Slavery* (San Francisco: Encounter Books, 2002).

23. Tony Martin, ed., "Eurocentric Attack," *Africana Studies at Wellesley Newsletter* 7 (1992), p. 2.

24. Frances S. Sayers, "Africana Studies Text Sparks Controversy," *Wellesley News,* 19 February 1993, pp. 1, 4.

25. As quoted in ibid., p. 4.

26. Ibid., p. 4.

27. In a speech at the University of Virginia in 1982 "Dr. Ben" was quoted as saying that the non-violence advocated by Dr. King was "just a strategy," and that he himself was a follower of Malcolm X; see David Snouffer, "Africa: Mother of History," *University Journal* 4, no. 47 (6 February 1982), p. 1.

28. On the strategy of maintaining a separate thought-world, see John H. McWhorter, *Losing the Race: Self-Sabotage in Black America* (New York: Free Press, 2000), pp. 54–55.

29. Minutes of the Senate meeting, 1 March 1993, pp. 2–3; Frances C.

Sayers, "Senate Discussion Covers Africana Studies, SBOG Advertisement," *Wellesley News,* 3 March 1993, p. 4.

30. Martin published a version of this speech in *Blacks and Jews at Wellesley News,* Broadside no. 1 (March 1993), pp. 1–4, from which the following quotations are taken.

31. Gates, "Black Demagogues."

32. Minutes of Academic Council, 4 March 1993.

33. Marcellus Andrews, "Andrews Reflects on Academic Freedom," *Wellesley News,* 14 April 1993, p. 13.

34. Nan Keohane, "Keohane Urges Freedom with Responsibility," *Wellesley News,* 10 March 1993, p. 14.

35. Selwyn Cudjoe, "Beyond Academic Freedom," *Wellesley News,* 24 March 1993, pp. 13–14.

36. Mary Lefkowitz, "Afrocentrists Wage War on Ancient Greeks," *Wall Street Journal,* 7 April 1993, p. A14.

37. Tony Martin, "Broadside no. 1" (March 1993). Copies of Martin's "Broadsides," including this one, have been posted on the Web site *Blacks and Jews Newspage* (www.blacksandjews.com).

38. Susan Bloch, "Furor at Wellesley College Over Anti-Semitic Text," *Boston Jewish Times* 48, no. 14 (1 April 1993), 1.

39. Spencer Blakeslee, *The Death of American Antisemitism* (Westport, Conn.: Praeger, 2000), p. 173.

40. Jerold Auerbach, "Anti-Semitism at Wellesley College," *Congress Monthly* (July–August 1993), p. 9.

41. Jack R. Fischel, "The New Anti-Semitic Axis: Holocaust Denial, Black Nationalism, and the Crisis on Our College Campuses," *Virginia Quarterly Review,* Spring 1995 (www.vqronline.org/viewmedia .php/prmMID/7483).

42. Moshe Y. Lewis, *History of Edom the Imposter Jew* (Brooklyn: MYL Publisher, 1989), pp. 17–18.

43. See also on ben-Jochannan's speech, above, this chapter.

44. Blakeslee, *Death of American Antisemitism,* p. 174, based on an interview, 5 July 1994.

45. Ibid., p. 175, based on an interview, 29 August 1995.

46. Ibid., p. 178, based on an interview, as above.

47. Chris Black, "Afro-centrist Wellesley Professor Rejects Charges that He Is Anti-Semitic," *Boston Globe,* 9 April 1993, p. 11; Lisa Sargent, "Jewish Groups Ask College to Review Martin's Tenure," *Wellesley News,* 14 April 1993, p. 1.

48. *Levin v. Harleston,* 986 F. 2nd 85 (2nd Cir. 1992): "Although appellants contended . . . that . . . Professor Levin's expression of his theories outside the classroom harmed the students and the educational process within the classroom, the district court saw no evidence that this was a factually valid concern. 770 F. Supp. at 922." See also Neil Hamilton, *Zealotry and Academic Freedom* (New Brunswick: Transaction Publishers, 1995), pp. 322–23.

FIVE
A New Anti-Semitism

1. Tony Martin, *The Jewish Onslaught: Despatches from the Wellesley Battlefront* (Dover, Mass.: The Majority Press, 1993); Spencer Blakeslee, *The Death of American Antisemitism* (Westport, Conn.: Praeger, 2000), p. 174.

2. Quoted by Chris Black, "Afro-centrist Wellesley Professor Rejects Charges that He Is Anti-Semitic," *Boston Globe,* 9 April 1993, p. 11.

3. *Blacks and Jews News* (published by the Historical Research Department of the Nation of Islam), Spring 1993, p. 4, and Autumn 1993, p. 4.

4. "Answering an Anti-Semite," *Boston Globe,* 2 February 1994, p. A12.

5. Martin, *The Jewish Onslaught,* pp. 3, 19.

6. Ibid., p. 64.

7. Ibid., p. 65.

8. Ibid., p. 30.

9. Ibid., p. 13.

10. Ibid., p. 68.

11. Diana Chapman Walsh, Letter to students, faculty, staff, alumnae, and friends of the College, 9 December 1993.

12. William Cain, e-mail re Tony Martin, 17 December 1993.

13. Martin, *Jewish Onslaught,* pp. 13, 39, 47–49, 75, and on Herodotus, pp. 60–62.

14. Mary Lefkowitz, "Combating False Theories in the Classroom," *Chronicle of Higher Education,* 19 January 1994, pp. B1–2.

15. *Jeffries v. Harleston,* 828 F. Supp. 1066 (SDNY 1993). Also see Cass R. Sunstein, *Democracy and the Problem of Free Speech* (New York: Free Press, 1993), pp. 204–8; Nathan Glazer, "Levin, Jeffries, and the Fate of Academic Autonomy," *Public Interest* 120 (Summer 1995), pp. 14–27.

16. See above, Chapter 4, after n. 28.

17. Richard Bernstein, *The Dictatorship of Virtue: Multiculturalism and the Battle for America's Future* (New York: Knopf, 1994), p. 118.

18. Alan Charles Kors and Harvey Silverglate, *The Shadow University: The Betrayal of Liberty on America's Campuses* (New York: Free Press, 1998), p. 105.

19. The names are listed in Guy MacLean Rogers, letter to the editor, *Wellesley News,* 2 March 1994, p. 11. Out of 223 faculty members, 124 signed, according to Alice Dembner, "Wellesley Faculty Joins Book Protest," *Boston Globe,* 17 March 1994, p. 29.

20. Bernstein, *Dictatorship of Virtue,* p. 119.

21. Dembner, "Wellesley Faculty."

22. Guy MacLean Rogers, "Controversial Courses at Wellesley," *Chronicle of Higher Education,* 8 June 1994, p. B4, and "Racism and Anti-semitism in the Classroom," *Midstream,* August–September 1994, pp. 8–10.

23. Alice Dembner, "Wellesley Denies Raise to Professor," *Boston Globe,* 26 August 1994, pp. A23, 28.

24. Jon Nordheimer, "Divided by a Diatribe; College Speech Ignites Furor Over Race," *New York Times,* 29 December 1993, p. B6: "Mr. Mu-

hammad at Kean was unsparing in attacking Jews and other whites. Often affecting a Jewish accent or effeminate mannerisms, he sprinkled phrases like 'Columbia Jew-niversity' and 'Jew York City' through a rambling three-hour talk billed as 'The Secret Relationship between Blacks and Jews.'" On Jeffries, see above, Chapter 4.

25. Tingha Apidta, "Garvey Scholar Rips *Jewish Onslaught*," *Blacks and Jews News* (Autumn 1993), pp. 2, 4.

26. Listing in an advertisement by EsoWon Books in the *Los Angeles Sentinel,* 13–19 January 1994. On black anti-Semitism in Chicago, see Paul M. Sniderman and Thomas Piazza, *Black Pride and Black Prejudice* (Princeton: Princeton University Press, 2002), pp. 77–90.

27. Steven A. Holmes, "Howard University Postponed Lecture by a Jewish Historian," *New York Times,* 16 April 1994, p. 9; Murray Friedman, *What Went Wrong? The Creation and Collapse of the Black-Jewish Alliance* (New York: Free Press, 1995), p. 346.

28. Martin cited as his source Harold David Brackman, "The Ebb and Flow of Conflict: A History of Black Jewish Relations Through 1900" (Ph.D. diss., University of California at Los Angeles, 1977); see vol. 1, p. 81. Brackman, however, had drawn his information not from the Babylonian Talmud itself but from a popular compilation of different rabbinic commentaries (see vol. 1, p. 131, n. 61). For detailed analysis of the origin of the Hamitic myth, see esp. Ephraim Isaac, "Genesis, Judaism, and the Sons of Ham," in *Slaves and Slavery in Muslim Africa,* ed. John Ralph Willis (Totowa, N.J.: Frank Cass, 1985), vol. 1, pp. 82–91.

29. See "Malik Zulu Shabazz in His Own Words," www.adl.org/Anti _semitism/shabazz.asp; "The Anti-Semitism of Professor Tony Martin in His Own Words," pamphlet (New York: Anti-Defamation League, 1996); also in "Documenting the Black Holocaust," C-Span Archives, 56177-1-DVD. See also Steven A. Holmes, "Howard University Is Stung by Images of Anti-Semitism," *New York Times,* 21 April 1994, pp. A1, D24.

30. Raymond A. Winbush, "Covering Up Hate Crimes on Campuses: A National Tragedy," *The Black Collegian* (First Semester Super Issue 1998), p. 152, citing personal correspondence from Martin dated 16 July 1998.

31. Nationwide Reporting Coverage, transcript of *Dr. Tony Martin, "Black Leaders Under Siege,"* 6 December 1994, pp. 68–69, 71. See also Lynne Meredith Cohn, "Editorial in Howard U. Paper Accuses ADL of Spying on Blacks," *Jewish News Weekly of Northern California,* 29 March 1996, quoting ADL Regional Director David Friedman (www.jewishsf.com/content/2-0-/module/displaystory/story_id/3273/edition_id/58/format/html/displaystory.html).

32. Chris Conner and Jacob W. Michaels, "Black, Jewish Students React to Martin's Speech," [University of Massachusetts at Amherst] *Daily Collegian,* 7 December 1994, pp. 1, 3; see also Tim White, "Controversial Lecture Fuels Student Debate," ibid., pp. 1, 3.

33. Robert Costrell, e-mail message to Mary Lefkowitz, 7 December 1994.

34. Bill Littman and Seth Stern, "Prof. Explains Views About Race Relations," *Cornell Daily Sun,* 2 May 1994, pp. 1.

SIX

Truth or Slander?

1. Mary Lefkowitz, "Hurt Feelings at Wellesley," *Measure* 118 (September–October 1993), pp. 1–6.

2. Avik S. Roy, "Afrocentric Scholar Accused of Harassment," *Counterpoint* 5, no. 1 (September 1993), pp. 6, 20.

3. Lefkowitz, "Hurt Feelings," p. 2.

4. Alyson Todd, "Blacks and Jews and All the News," *Heterodoxy* (May–June 1993), p. 5, reprinted in *The Heterodoxy Handbook: How to Survive the PC Campus,* ed. David Horowitz and Peter Collier (Washington: Regnery Publishing, 1994), pp. 152–55.

5. Sunita Subramanian, Julie Provost, and Jennifer J. Paull, "Inter-

views with Professor Anthony Martin and Student Michelle Plantec," *Galenstone,* issue 5 (May 1993), pp. 8–10. See Chapter 1.

6. Spencer Blakeslee, *The Death of American Antisemitism* (Westport,
   Conn.: Praeger, 2000), p. 177.

7. Michelle Plantec, letter to Ms. [Emily] Tobin of the ACLU, 8 March
   1992.

SEVEN

Reparations?

1. *Martin v. Lefkowitz,* 1994 Mass. Super. at Middlesex; LEXIS 37, C.A.
   93–7454; appeal, *Martin v. Lefkowitz,* Mass. C.A. 94-P-001944.

2. *Martin v. Lefkowitz,* Mass. C.A. 93–7454, 18 October 1996, Deposition of Anthony Martin: Exhibit #3.

3. Telephone interview with the author, August 1996. I found out
   about the Toledo offer to Martin from Sandra Stotsky, a research
   associate at the Harvard Graduate School of Education. Stotsky in
   turn learned about it from a friend in Ohio who was acquainted
   with Freeman-Smith.

4. Mindy Nierenburg, Statement written at the request of Gwenn
   Bookman, 13 November 1991; Juliet Salzman, letter to whom it
   may concern, 14 November 1991; Sarah A. Crain, letter to Gwenn
   Bookman, 14 November 1991.

5. Margaret Cezair-Thompson, Jodi Mikalachki, Jean Stanley, Wel-
   lington Nyangoni, Lynn Hampton (class of 1992), Adlai Murdoch,
   and Tony Martin, Memo to Nan Keohane and Molly Campbell, 6
   November 1991.

6. *Martin v. Lefkowitz,* Mass. C.A. 93–7454, 12–20–96, Deposition of
   Mary Lefkowitz: Exhibit #5.

7. *Martin v. Lefkowitz,* Mass. C.A. 93–7454, docket entry MICV93–
   07454B.

8. *Martin v. Lefkowitz,* 46 Mass. App. Ct. 1127 (1999); 710 N.E. 2d 242;
   1999 Mass. App. LEXIS 571, C.A. 98-P-723 (1999).

9. Tony Martin, *Blacks and Jews at Wellesley News,* Broadside no. 4 (March 1998), p. 1. Copies of Martin's "Broadsides" are posted on the Web site *Blacks and Jews Newspage* (www.blacksandjews.com). The site also contains articles with titles like "Bush and the U.S. government implicated in 9/11; Muslims HAD NO PART IN IT! Filmed PROOF!" and "Min. Farrakah Implicates Israel in Iraq War, Photos Prove It," and "Obtain your copy of the most controversial book in America, *The Secret Relationship Between Blacks and Jews,* vol. 1."

10. *Martin v. Roy,* 9 Mass. L. Rep. 522 (Sup. Ct. 1998) 27 Media L. Rep. 1942, C.A. 93–07137 (1998); Julie Nicklin, "Wellesley Professor Fails to Prove Libel Against Student," *Chronicle of Higher Education,* 15 January 1999, p. A16.

11. *Martin v. Roy,* 54 Mass. App. Ct. 642; 767 N.E. 2d 603 (2002), C.A. 99-P-1649 (2002).

12. Courtney Leatherman, "Controversial Scholar Loses Race-Bias Suit Against Wellesley College," *Chronicle of Higher Education,* 18 June 1999, p. A16.

13. Mari J. Matsuda, Charles R. Lawrence, III, Richard Delgado, and Kimberlè Williams Crenshaw, *Words That Wound: Critical Race Theory, Assaultive Speech, and the First Amendment* (Boulder: Westview Press, 1993), pp. 8–9.

14. See esp. Samuel Walker, *Hate Speech: The History of an American Controversy* (Lincoln: University of Nebraska Press, 1994), pp. 139–41.

15. James B. Jacobs and Kimberly Potter, *Hate Crimes: Criminal Law and Identity Politics* (New York: Oxford University Press, 1998), p. 199. The University of Wisconsin's speech code was abolished in 1999; see the detailed account in Donald Alexander Downs, *Restoring Free Speech and Liberty on Campus* (Cambridge: Independent Institute/Cambridge University Press, 2005), pp. 190–257.

EIGHT

A Racist Polemic?

1. Jean Terrasson, *Séthos, histoire ou vie* (Paris: Jacques Guerin, 1731); English translation, *Life of Sethos,* tr. by Thomas Lediard (London: J. Walthoe, 1732).

2. For more details, see Mary Lefkowitz, *Not Out of Africa: How Afrocentrism Became an Excuse to Teach Myth as History* (New York: Basic Books, 1996, 1997), pp. 110–21.

3. On Champollion's visit to Egypt, see Lesley and Roy Adkins, *The Keys of Egypt: The Obsession to Decipher Egyptian Hieroglyphics* (New York: HarperCollins Publishers, 2000), pp. 242–79.

4. Lefkowitz, *Not Out of Africa.*

5. On the strategy, see Paul R. Gross and Norman Levitt, *Higher Superstition: The Academic Left and Its Quarrels with Science* (Baltimore: Johns Hopkins University Press, 1994), p. 8.

6. Selwyn R. Cudjoe, "Not a Racist Polemic . . . ," *Boston Sunday Globe,* 21 April 1996, p. 85.

7. Mary Lefkowitz, "Afrocentrism Poses a Threat to the Rationalist Tradition," *Chronicle of Higher Education,* 6 May 1992, p. A52 (see Chapter 3, at n. 10).

8. On the various negative terms used by postmodernists to characterize arguments based on warranted evidence, see Barbara S. Held, *Psychology's Interpretive Turn* (Washington: American Psychological Association, 2007), p. 27.

9. Alice Dembner, "Afrocentrism Debated at Wellesley Teach-In," *Boston Globe,* 2 May 1996, p. 87.

10. On the use of "possibilities," see esp. Harry G. Frankfurt, *On Bullshit* (Princeton: Princeton University Press, 2005), pp. 61–62; for further examples, see Barbara S. Held, *Back to Reality: A Critique of Postmodern Theory in Psychotherapy* (New York: W. W. Norton, 1995), pp. 94–102.

11. Cudjoe, "Not a Racist Polemic."

12. Dembner, "Afrocentrism Debated."

13. On the question of identity-based "knowledge," see esp. Jonathan Rauch, *Kindly Inquisitors: The New Attacks on Free Thought* (Chicago: University of Chicago Press, 1993), pp. 145–47; Martha C. Nussbaum, *Cultivating Humanity: A Classical Defense of Reform in Liberal Education* (Cambridge: Harvard University Press, 1997), p. 174.

14. Punning on Jewish names was one of Muhammad's favorite tropes; see the note on his speech at Kean College in Chapter 5. In a speech at San Francisco State University on 21 May 1997 Muhammad observed: "Stealberg, they call him Stealberg. When it's Swindler's list, they call it Schindler's list." Quotation from "Khalid Abdul Muhammad In His Own Words" on the ADL Web site, www.adl.org/special_reports/khalid_own_words/on_jewish_control.asp.

15. On Afrocentric homophobia, see Clarence E. Walker, *We Can't Go Home Again: An Argument about Afrocentrism* (New York: Oxford University Press, 2001), pp. 122–23.

16. Robert S. Boynton, "The Bernaliad: A Scholar-Warrior's Long Journey to Ithaca," *Lingua Franca,* November 1996, p. 43.

17. George F. Will, "Intellectual Segregation," *Newsweek,* 19 February 1996, p. 78.

18. Mary R. Lefkowitz and Guy MacLean Rogers, eds., *Black Athena Revisited* (Chapel Hill: University of North Carolina Press, 1996); see Chapter 9. Some people assumed I was a conservative because I had asked for and received small grants from the Bradley and Olin Foundations to help support the modest salaries of the students who had worked on *Not Out of Africa.* No one seemed to have noticed that in *Black Athena Revisited,* a critique of Bernal's volumes 1 and 2 that Guy Rogers and I edited together in 1996, we also thanked the liberal Ford Foundation for its assistance with the publication.

19. Christopher Stray, review in *Journal of Hellenic Studies* 117 (1997), 229–31.

20. David Konstan, "Inventing Ancient Greece," *History and Theory* 36, no. 2 (May 1997), p. 269.

21. Wilson Jeremiah Moses, *Afrotopia: The Roots of African American Popular History* (Cambridge Studies in American History and Culture 118, ed. Eric Sundquist; Cambridge: Cambridge University Press, 1998), pp. 8–9.

22. Ibid., p. 36.

23. Walker, *We Can't Go Home*, p. xxiv, quoting Wilson J. Moses, "In Fairness to Afrocentrism," in *Alternatives to Afrocentrism*, ed. John J. Miller (New York: Center for the New American Community/ Manhattan Institute, 1994), p. 21. See also Glenn Loury, "Color Blinded," *Arion* N.S. 4, no. 2 (1997), 171–72.

24. See esp. Jim Sleeper, *Liberal Racism* (New York: Viking, 1997), pp. 18–19.

25. Moses, *Afrotopia*, p. 7.

26. Rauch, *Kindly Inquisitors*, pp. 125–31. See also the discussion of "words that wound" in Chapter 7, at n. 13 and following.

NINE
Turning History into Fiction

1. Martin Bernal, *Black Athena: The Afroasiatic Roots of Classical Civilization*, vols. 1 and 2 (Rutgers, N.J.: Rutgers University Press, 1987, 1991).

2. See esp. Jay H. Jasanoff and Alan Nussbaum, "Word Games: The Linguistic Evidence in *Black Athena*," in *Black Athena Revisited*, ed. Mary R. Lefkowitz and Guy MacLean Rogers (Chapel Hill: University of North Carolina Press, 1996), pp. 177, quoting from Bernal's review of Lefkowitz, *Not Out of Africa*, http://ccat.sas .upenn.edu/bmcr/1996/96.04.05.html, reprinted, with revisions, in Martin Bernal, *Black Athena Writes Back* (Durham, N.C.: Duke University Press, 2001), see esp. pp. 382, 393–95.

3. On the technique, see Paul R. Gross and Norman Levitt, *Higher Superstition: The Academic Left and Its Quarrels with Science* (Baltimore: Johns Hopkins University Press, 1994), p. 8.

4. Ibid., pp. 4–5.
5. The fiction of a progressive Bernal versus a conservative establishment was maintained also by Judaic studies professor Jacques Berlinerblau in his account of the *Black Athena* controversy, *Heresy in the University* (New Brunswick, N.J.: Rutgers University Press, 1999).
6. *BA* I, pp. 1, 3.
7. "To be accepted as a paradigm, a theory must *seem* [italics mine] better than its competitors; that is, it must *work*"; T. S. Kuhn, *The Structure of Scientific Revolutions,* 2nd ed. (Chicago: University of Chicago Press, 1970), p. 17, see also p. 208. On Kuhn's apparent reluctance to acknowledge the existence of objective reality, see David Stove, *The Plato Cult and Other Philosophical Follies* (Oxford: Blackwell, 1991), pp. 8–11.
8. An accepted postmodernist approach is to argue that authenticity is culturally based; see, for example, the article on Lefkowitz, *Not Out of Africa,* by Joanne Monteagle Stearns, "Jargon, Authenticity, and the Nature of Cultural History Writing," *Ancient Art and Its Historiography,* ed. A. A. Donohue and Mark D. Fullerton (Cambridge: Cambridge University Press, 2003), pp. 171–201.
9. Gross and Levitt, *Flight from Science,* p. 6. See also Daniel A. Farber and Suzanna Sherry, *Beyond All Reason: The Radical Assault on Truth in American Law* (New York: Oxford University Press, 1997), p. 40; Donald Alexander Downs, *Restoring Free Speech and Liberty on Campus* (Cambridge: Independent Institute/Cambridge University Press, 2005), pp. 48–49.
10. *BA* I, pp. 179–81.
11. For more details, see Mary Lefkowitz, *Not Out of Africa: How Afrocentrism Became an Excuse to Teach Myth as History* (New York: Basic Books, 1997), pp. 93–94, 110–21.
12. Mary R. Lefkowitz and Guy MacLean Rogers, eds., *Black Athena Revisited* (Chapel Hill: University of North Carolina Press, 1996).
13. In ibid.: John Baines, "The Aims and Methods of *Black Athena,*"

pp. 27–48; David O'Connor, "Egypt and Greece: The Bronze Age Evidence," pp. 49–61; Frank J. Yurco, "An Egyptological Review," pp. 62–100.

14. In Lefkowitz and Rogers, eds., *Black Athena Revisited:* Kathryn A. Bard, "Ancient Egyptians and the Issue of Race," pp. 103–11; Frank M. Snowden, Jr., "Bernal's 'Blacks' and the Afrocentrists," pp. 112–28; C. Loring Brace, et al., "Clines and Clusters vs. 'Race,'" pp. 129–64.

15. Jasanoff and Nussbaum, "Word Games," pp. 177–205.

16. Ibid., p. 201. Bernal has now published a third volume, *Black Athena: The Linguistic Evidence* (New Brunswick, N.J.: Rutgers University Press, 2006). According to the publisher's blurb, the book addresses the central question raised by *Stolen Legacy:* "Could Greek philosophy be rooted in Egyptian thought?" The idea that such a question could be answered by linguistics goes back to Senegalese scientist Cheikh Anta Diop (1923–86), one of the founding fathers of Afrocentrism. Diop maintained that Egyptian was the mother language from which all others derived, including Wolof and even ancient Greek; see the charts in his *Civilization or Barbarism: An Authentic African Anthropology,* tr. Yaa-Lengi Meema Ngemi et al. (Chicago: Lawrence Hill Books, 1991), pp. 358–61, 379; analysis in François-Xavier Fauvelle, *L'Afrique de Cheikh Anta Diop* (Paris: Karthala, 1996), pp. 162–65, and Henry Tourneux, "L'argument linguistique chez Cheikh Anta Diop et ses disciples," in *Afrocentrismes,* ed. François-Xavier Fauvelle-Aymar, Jean-Pierre Chrétien, and Claude-Hélène Perrot (Paris: Karthala, 2000), pp. 88–99. Diop's etymologies appear to be based entirely on supposed similarities in sound. Ancient Greeks and Romans made connections between words that sounded alike in order to determine the words' "true" (*etymos*) meaning. But the procedure has no scientific value, and is eschewed by modern linguists; see Pascal Vernus, "Situation de l'égyptien dans les langues du monde," in *Afrocentrismes,* ed. Fauvelle-Aymar et al., p. 196.

In any case etymology does not have any real bearing on the question of whether Egyptian thought had any significant influence on Greek philosophy. Even if it could be shown that many Greek words derived from ancient Egyptian, one would need to demonstrate that there were extensive similarities between early Egyptian and Greek philosophical works. But no works of Egyptian philosophy appear to have existed before the early centuries A.D., long after the founding of Alexandria and Greek political domination of Egypt.

Undaunted by such unpromising realities, Bernal tries to make a case for "massive" Egyptian influence by listing related groups of "plausible" etymologies. None of these etymologies is likely to carry much conviction among professional linguists, not because linguists are prejudiced in any way against the possibility of Egyptian origins, but because Bernal has made use of so many ad hoc and exceptional arguments in order to construct them. Each of Bernal's etymologies appears to be based on a perceived similarity of sound and then contrived and custom-tailored in order to give a desired result. Because Bernal is so determined to find close links between Egypt and Greece, he never appears to allow for the possibility of derivations from Minoan or one of the other lost Aegean languages or to call attention to the fact that Egyptian borrowings in Greek conform to consistent rules, and their connections with their Egyptian counterparts can easily be established; see Jasanoff and Nussbaum, "Word Games," pp. 188–89.

For an example of the problems involved in Bernal's attempts to concoct etymologies, let us consider the possible etymology of a distinctive Greek word that is central to his argument, *philosophia*. The word is made up of two components, *philo-* (loving) and *sophia* (wisdom). Neither has a certain Indo-European origin. Bernal attempts to derive both components from Egyptian, though of course they might each have come from some lost regional language or languages. He argues (vol. 3, p. 206) that Greek *phil-* derives from

Egyptian *mri,* with *m* theoretically representing a nasal form of the labials *b, p, ph,* and with *r* and *l* considered to be interchangeable. Elsewhere, when it suits its purpose, Bernal suggests that Greek *ph* derives from Egyptian *f;* see Jasanoff and Nussbaum, "Word Games," p. 199. In known borrowings from Egyptian the sounds of Egyptian words tend to come into Greek unchanged; see ibid., pp. 188–89.

Although in the case of *phil-* Bernal argues that *ph* represents an Egyptian *m,* in the case of the root *soph-* he argues that the *ph* comes not from Egyptian *m* or even *f* but *b* in the root *sb3* (where *3* represents an unknown vowel sound or indeed its absence). But in reality all that the Greek roots *soph-* and Coptic *sb3* have in common is the initial sound *s,* something that is true of a great many other unrelated words. The short *o* of *sophos* does not occur in the Coptic derivatives of *sb3,* such as *sabe/sbō* (wise person/ wisdom). These latter two late Egyptian derivatives share some aspects of the semantic field of Greek *sophos,* but their meanings would have been distinct in the second millennium B.C., at the time when Bernal supposes that a large number of Egyptian words were incorporated into Greek: the Egyptian root *sb3* denotes teaching, while the basic meaning of Greek *sophos* is "clever, skilled."

Bernal also tries to use etymologies to shore up another side of his crumbling edifice, namely, his argument that Greeks like Herodotus were justified in supposing that Greek religious customs and ideas derived from Egypt. Complex etymologies would supposedly confirm that Herodotus knew what he was talking about when he said "the names of almost all the gods come from Egypt" (*Histories* 2.50). But the Egyptologist Jan Assmann offers a much more elegant explanation: When Egyptian priests guided Herodotus around Egyptian religious sites, "they did not speak to him of Amun, Re, Thoth, Osiris, etc., but used the Greek versions of their names"; *Weisheit und Mysterium: Das Bild der Griechen von Ägypten* (Munich: C. H. Beck, 2000), p. 32.

17. In Lefkowitz and Rogers, eds., *Black Athena Revisited:* Robert Palter, "*Black Athena,* Afrocentrism, and the History of Science," pp. 209–66.

18. In Lefkowitz and Rogers, eds., *Black Athena Revisited:* Emily Vermeule, "The World Turned Upside Down," p. 178; Sarah P. Morris, "The Legacy of *Black Athena,*" pp. 167–74; Vermeule, "World Turned Upside Down," pp. 169–79; John E. Coleman, "Did Egypt Shape the Glory That Was Greece," pp. 280–302; Lawrence A. Tritle, "*Black Athena:* Vision or Dream of Greek Origins?" pp. 303–30.

19. In Lefkowitz and Rogers, eds., *Black Athena Revisited:* Edith Hall, "When Is a Myth Not a Myth," pp. 333–48.

20. In Lefkowitz and Rogers, eds., *Black Athena Revisited:* Robert Palter, "Eighteenth-Century Historiography in *Black Athena,*" pp. 349–402.

21. In Lefkowitz and Rogers, eds., *Black Athena Revisited:* Richard Jenkyns, "Bernal and the Nineteenth Century," pp. 411–20; Mario Liverani, "The Bathwater and the Baby," pp. 421–27.

22. In Lefkowitz and Rogers, eds., *Black Athena Revisited:* Robert E. Norton, "The Tyranny of Germany over Greece?" pp. 403–10; on Grote, see Guy MacLean Rogers, "Multiculturalism and the Foundations of Western Civilization," pp. 430–34.

23. Rogers, "Multiculturalism and the Foundations," pp. 442–43. For a more detailed summary of *Black Athena Revisited,* see Guy MacLean Rogers, "Quo Vadis?" in *Black Athena Revisited,* ed. Lefkowitz and Rogers, pp. 447–53.

24. Josine H. Blok, "Proof and Persuasion in *Black Athena* I: The Case of K. O. Müller," in *Black Athena: Ten Years After,* ed. Wim M. J. van Binsbergen, *Talanta* 28–29 (1996–97), pp. 173–208.

25. Alan Sokal, "Transgressing the Boundaries: Towards a Transformative Hermeneutics of Quantum Gravity," *Social Text* 46/47 (1996), pp. 217–52.

26. For a copy of the article and discussion of what it was parodying, see Alan Sokal and Jean Bricmont, *Fashionable Nonsense: Postmodern*

Intellectuals' Abuse of Science (New York: Picador, 1998); Editors of *Lingua Franca,* eds., *The Sokal Hoax: The Sham That Shook the Academy* (Lincoln: University of Nebraska Press, 2000).

27. Alan D. Sokal, "A Physicist Experiments with Cultural Studies," originally published in *Lingua Franca,* May–June 1996, pp. 62, reprinted in Editors of *Lingua Franca, Sokal Hoax,* pp. 49–58; also available at www.physics.nyu.edu/faculty/sokal/#papers.

28. Michael Bellesiles, *Arming America* (New York: Knopf, 2000).

29. Peter Charles Hoffer, *Past Imperfect: Facts, Fictions, and Fraud in the Writing of American History* (New York: Basic Books, 2004), p. 143.

30. Ibid., p. 150.

31. Ibid., p. 156.

32. Ron Robin, *Scandals and Scoundrels: Seven Cases That Shook The Academy* (Berkeley: University of California Press, 2004), p. 63.

33. Hoffer, *Past Imperfect,* p. 166; Robin, *Scandals and Scoundrels,* pp. 76–77.

34. See, for example, Jon Wiener, *Historians in Trouble* (New York: The New Press: 2005), p. 93: "If he had published research showing that there were fewer books in early America than previously believed, rather than fewer guns, he might be wrong, but he'd still be teaching at Emory."

35. Bernal, *BA* II, pp. xvi–xvii.

36. Blok, "Proof and Persuasion," p. 208.

37. On the question of Cleopatra's ethnicity, see Lefkowitz, *Not Out of Africa,* pp. 45–51.

Epilogue

1. Wilson Jeremiah Moses, *Afrotopia: The Roots of African American Popular History* (Cambridge Studies in American History and Culture 118, ed. Eric Sundquist; Cambridge: Cambridge University Press, 1998), p. 8 (discussed in Chapter 8).

2. Selwyn R. Cudjoe, "Not a Racist Polemic . . . ," *Boston Sunday Globe,* 21 April 1996, p. 85 (discussed in Chapter 8).

3. For examples, see the anecdotal evidence in David K. Shipler, *A Country of Strangers: Blacks and Whites in America* (New York: Alfred A. Knopf, 1997), pp. 188–226.

4. Austin Fenner, "Prof: Black History Got Start in Egypt," *New York Daily News,* 13 February 2005, p. 28.

5. Tony Martin, "Black Studies at Wellesley," *Encyclopedia of Black Studies,* ed. Molefi Kete Asante and Ama Mazama (Thousand Oaks: Sage Publications, 2005), pp. 160–64. Cf. also Kenneth J. Cooper, "A Tenure Not Soon Forgotten," *Diverse Issues in Higher Education* 24, no. 7 (17 May 2007), p. 12.

6. Jim Sleeper, *Liberal Racism* (New York: Viking, 1997), p. 19.

7. John McWhorter, *Winning the Race: Beyond the Crisis in Black America* (New York: Gotham Books, 2005), p. 6.

8. Martha Nussbaum, *The Clash Within: Violence, Democracy, and India's Future* (Cambridge: Harvard University Press, 2007), pp. 224–27, 237–44.

9. Ibid., p. 258.

10. Ibid., pp. 253, 255.

11. Ibid., p. 262; also Martha C. Nussbaum, *Cultivating Humanity: A Classical Defense of Reform in Liberal Education* (Cambridge: Harvard University Press, 1997), p. 185.

12. Nussbaum, *The Clash Within,* p. 239.

13. See Chapter 9.

14. Wellesley College Student Senate Minutes, 1 March 1993, p. 3.

15. See Chapter 3, at n. 3.

16. Matthew Purdy, "New Jersey Laureate Refuses to Resign over Poem," *New York Times,* 26 September 2002, p. B1; see also Maria Newman, "Poet Laureate Stands by Words Against Israel and Won't Step Down," *New York Times,* 3 October 2002, p. B8.

17. For a list of some of these claims, see Anti-Defamation League, "Sep-

tember 11 and Arab Media: The Anti-Jewish and Anti-American Blame Game," www.adl.org/911/ArabMedia_911.pdf.

18. For all quotations, and the basic account of the event, see Jenna Russell, "Poet Baraka Met by Charges of Anti-Semitism at Wellesley," *Boston Globe,* 24 November 2002, p. B3.

19. Lawrence D. Lowenthal, "The Proof *Baraka* Seems to Need," *Boston Globe,* 30 November 2002, p. A14.

20. When Tony Martin was paid two thousand dollars to lecture at Worcester State College, trustee Roberta Schaefer resigned in protest; see Jon Auerbach, "College Roiled by Slated Lecture, Worcester Trustee Resigns in Protest," *Boston Globe,* 23 January 1995, Metro p. 15; *Chronicle of Higher Education,* 23 February 1995.

Acknowledgments

I t will be clear from the course of this narrative that at times
I have been the teacher, at other times a student again,
struggling hard to find my way in unfamiliar territory. I
could not have survived without the help of my family and
friends. Some of their names are mentioned in the text, but I am
particularly grateful to Sir Hugh Lloyd-Jones for his encourage-
ment and sharp criticism, to the late Frank M. Snowden, Jr.,
for his moral support, and to Barbara Held for valuable advice
during all these years. My agents Lynn Chu and Glen Hartley
encouraged me to write this book and helped me at every stage of
the process. Lauren Brownlee, Dee Clayman, Margery Lucas, and
Martha Nussbaum each read drafts of the whole text and made
many improvements. Robin Akert, Tom Burke, Stanley Katz, and

Lynne Viti commented on individual chapters. Jay Jasanoff and Joshua Katz have generously helped me with my discussions of linguistic issues.

I owe special thanks also to people whom I came to know in the course of my journey. These include the Greeks and Americans of Greek descent who have studied ancient history and understand why I was concerned about what was being taught in schools and universities in this country. And I am deeply grateful to the many people of African descent who wrote to me and told me that they understood what I was trying to do, and who encouraged me to keep on doing it.

My brother John Rosenthal, to whom this book is dedicated, never failed to take a keen interest in all that was going on. If only he were still alive, and we could go on talking, as we did throughout the nineties, about all these issues.

Index